Psalms of the Daughter

Lynn Pinder

TAKE ACTION! Publishing
www.takeactionpublishing.com
Baltimore, Maryland

Published by TAKE ACTION! Publishing, a project of The TAKE ACTION! Network (www.thetakeactionnetwork.com), and a subsidiary of Create- A-Book BALTIMORE.

ISBN 13:   978-0-6151-4410-8
Library of Congress Cataloging-In-Publication Data Pending

Bible excerpts used throughout this book are from www.biblegateway.com.

"A Biblical Response: Psalm 2" was not written by the author and was excerpted from 1 Corinthians 13:1-13 (The Message).

The poem, "I Thought You Would Be The One," was written by the author and was originally published in Songs of Hope (Timeless Avatar Press, 2006).

The song, "Oh, It Is Jesus," was written by Andrae Crouch and originally performed by Andrae Crouch, Myra Walker, and Teta Vega.

The words, "The Place that Seems Like the End is Only the Beginning," were written by someone other than the author and was originally published by a greeting card company as a verse on the front cover of a note card.

The paragraph, "I miss you. I miss your presence and I miss the freedom of knowing that I can be with you. To be honest, I began to miss you as I walked away from you, but I was too stubborn too admit it to myself. A man's silly pride can make him do silly things. But whatever happens, I just don't want to lose you. I never would have imagined that in such a short period of time, you could mean so much to me...imagine that. Today is Memorial Day and I just want to be where you are," was written by someone other than the author and was excerpted from a handwritten note card.

For orders in bulk, please contact TAKE ACTION! Publishing.
www.takeactionpublishing.com
1-800-929-1418

Acknowledgments

I cannot even begin to thank all the people who have helped to make this book project a reality. From your prayers to your words of encouragement to your unexpected acts of kindness, I am just so grateful to have all of you (family, friends, former co-workers, current co-workers, church members, neighbors, god-mothers, pastors, mentors, and prayer warriors) in my life.

I am extremely thankful for my immediate and extended family, but I am especially grateful to my sisters – Sherri, Angie, Regina, and Deon; my Step-Mom – Delores Pinder; my Aunt - Barbara Brown; my Grandfathers - Joseph Pinder and Junius "Paul" Thomas; and my Restoring Life International Church family.

I want to thank Peter Guttmacher and Raina Moore for their patience and honest feedback during the editing process. Also, I need to thank Vernell Hightower for her honest critique, and Anita "Kenyeme" Phillips for her help with the final revision. Finally, I extend my sincerest thanks to everyone who purchased copies of this book. I appreciate your support!

I dedicate this book to the loving memory of my birth mother – Bertha Ann Jones Vaughn Pinder; my father – Leon Reginald Pinder; my grandmothers – Louise Johnson, Charlotte Louise Thomas, and Annie Mae Williams; and my unnamed one.

"Your word is a lamp to my feet and a light for my path."
- Psalm 119:105 (NIV)

Psalms of the Daughter

Psalms of the Daughter

CONTENTS

CHAPTER ONE
SEARCHING

"My eyes fail from
searching Your word, Saying, 'When will You comfort me?'"
- Psalm 119:82 (NKJV)

Closure

"I like to visit her. Lingering in her shadow, I live as a dark moment - a faded memory of what was and a soft reminder of what may never be. I exist to rouse in her guilt and shame from hushed taboos wrapped in whispered secrets of years long past. Sometimes I think she feels I'm near, but other times I know she doesn't recognize my presence. She is the mother. I took the child long ago, and I won't stop until I take her life, too."
--the adversary

It seemed like an eternity since that dreadful day when Shawna had the abortion, and she still struggled with bouts of depression over the decision that had scarred her life. She had been only sixteen at the time and felt like her whole world was crashing down on her. And she never forgave herself – always feeling like she should have done more to save the little life that once grew inside of her. The feeling resonated into a sadness that stirred in Shawna's soul and touched every person who met her; it was in her eyes. When people met Shawna, they wondered about the sadness that lingered there. Few knew it stemmed from her knowing - somehow - that she had ended the only life that would ever come from her.

"She's vulnerable."
"I know. She almost succumbed to our pressure."
"We need to stay on her. She is a special case."
"We must make certain that she is never set free."
"Yes, we want self-doubt, bitterness, sorrow, and condemnation to wear her down until she forgets her destiny."
--legion

Sitting behind her imported mahogany desk, Shawna swiveled around to look out the oversized window of her upscale, downtown office. Watching the pedestrians dance their way through the heavy afternoon traffic, she sighed. Today was an anniversary of sorts for her. As she leaned back in her chair, images of her teen angst whirled through her mind.

*   *   *

Eleven months had passed since that rainy day when Shawna had had the procedure; and, ironically, she had started a part-time job in the same building where it took place. On this particular Saturday as Shawna's sister dropped her off at work, the tiny parking lot was a buzz with protestors who first swarmed the car and then Shawna as she struggled to make her way to the front entrance of the building. The protestors – a mix of middle-aged men and women - hoisted signs and shouts toward Shawna as they pleaded for her to save the life they thought was growing inside of her.

"Don't kill your baby!" screamed one lady behind Shawna.

"Please, you don't have to do this!" another lady shouted as she tugged at Shawna's hand.

Shawna snatched her hand away from the woman's grasp. Feeling a bit woozy, she quickened her pace as she tried desperately to make her way through all of the commotion to the building's tinted glass doors. Shawna wasn't sure if it was her facial expression or the woman tugging at her arm that alarmed her sister.

"L-E-A-V-E H-E-R A-L-O-N-E!" her sister screamed repeatedly out of the car window at the protestors.

Overwhelmed by the chaos, Shawna ran full speed into the building. Once inside the dimly lit lobby, she glanced over her shoulder out of the tinted glass doors just in time to see her sister - with tears streaming down her face - back the car she was driving out of the parking lot. Shawna gazed dazedly at the protestors who lingered seemingly in wait for their next wounded soul. Her mind drifted back to that rainy day eleven months earlier when she had in fact visited the clinic for the very thing that the protestors feared. The tweet of the elevator chime brought her attention back to the present situation. As three uniformed officers stepped off the elevator, Shawna quickly wiped the tears from her eyes and turned to face them. Watching her intently, the officers inquired of her destination. After having determined that Shawna was indeed an employee in the building, they escorted her to the little office three floors below the abortion clinic where she worked until she graduated high school.

*   *   *

And here Shawna was - thirteen years later - still wounded by the memory of it all. A successful corporate executive, she couldn't help but wonder if her life would have been different if those protesters had been present on that rainy day when she had first gone to the clinic. Shawna wondered if the protesters' presence would have impacted her decision to end the life that was growing inside of her. A decision which, although she felt pressured into making, was ultimately her own. The question nagged at her heart. And even now years later, the thought burdened her soul. As Shawna eased her chair back from the desk, she stood and stretched. Her eyes watered over and as the tears flowed briskly down her face, Shawna lifted a heart-felt plea to the Lord.

"Please forgive me, God. I apologize for aborting the precious life you chose me to birth. Oh Lord, please forgive me! Help me to forgive myself and help me to forgive those whom I felt let me down when I needed them most. I know this has been a difficult burden for them, too. God, please loose this from our spirits. Release this burden from our hearts. I feel so empty and alone. Lord God, I need you. I need you to help me push pass this pain. I need you to help me thrive in your grace. God, help me to walk in the purpose you have predestined for my life."

-God's daughter

"Finally my daughter, it has taken you so long to seek me. I AM here. I was there with you on that rainy day. I was with the nurse as she held your hand and wiped your tears. I was with you in the recovery room as you lay on the cot in shock trying to forget the horrific sound of it all. I was there in that room with you and all the other women – young, old, black, and white – who made the same choice as you. I was with you that day in the parking lot when you encountered the protestors. Beloved, I am with you now. I have always been with you - waiting for you to choose me. You must trust that I have all things in control - even this, my daughter."

--GOD

"Oh no, she is praying!"

-legion

"Stay on her. We must continue to press her and feed that root of bitterness in her heart so that she remains bound in guilt and shame."

--the adversary

"Get back satan! You have no power over her."
                                                           --GOD

Shawna, standing on the plush carpet in front of the oversized window, felt the warmth of the sun kiss her raised forehead as she surrendered her damaged soul to God. Overcome by the Holy Spirit, she fell to her knees and wept uncontrollably.

                    *   *   *

Having just returned from her lunch break, Shawna's secretary poked her head into Shawna's office only to observe her boss kneeled in what looked like prayer in front of the oversized window. She gently shut the door and walked back to her desk. If anyone inquired of Shawna's whereabouts, she knew to inform them that her boss was in an important meeting with top management.

My Prayer

God, I need you!
You are my refuge and strength.

I know I should not be afraid,
but I am.

I know I should rely on your will,
but my faith is wavering.

I know I should stand still
and trust that You are God,
but I'm still searching.

I'm searching for my way.
I'm searching for salvation.
I'm searching for comfort.

Help me, Lord!
Help me to be still and know that You are God!
Help me to trust in Your Word
and to walk in Your truth and light.

A Restless Spirit

I'm missing you so much it hurts.
It's been long enough for me to be over you.
Yet, you are very much still a part of me.
I try to shake you thinking maybe,
Just maybe the feelings will go away
But they don't.
So, I try to accept the fact that I still love you.

But it's no easier and the loneliness engulfs me.
I can still hear you whispering my name.
I can still see your gigantic smile and that sparkle in your eyes.
I can still feel your touch.
And as I close my eyes,
I can remember how easy it was to lose myself in you.

I remember those long conversations that just seemed to flow effortlessly.
I remember how natural it seemed for me to love you.
I remember sitting next to you asking God if you were the one.
I remember the day I realized how much I wanted you to be him.
I was so overwhelmed with your presence.
You touched every part of me and challenged me in every way.

My spirit is unbearably heavy,
As my mind begins to relive every moment
I ever spent with you.
I sigh in desperation begging God to move me out of this place.
And as I sit quietly,
I pray for guidance.
I pray for increased faith.
I pray for wisdom.
I pray for happiness.
I pray for peace.
I pray for the courage to let go and let God work things out.
I pray for the patience to wait on Him to release His perfect will in my life.

The Body

The air was tight and as humid as is expected on an August night in Baltimore. The night shadows made it almost impossible for the one holding the gun to see the face of the one kneeling before him, but he knew the man was crying.

"Fool, you can at least die like a man and stop crying like a b-----!"

That was the only response that the shooter would utter before taking the life of the young man. One clean shot to the back of the head was all it took. The impact of the bullet shattered the man's skull as he fell limp to the ground. And as the shooter returned his gun to its holster, he realized how much he hated Leakin Park. Still, he knew that this was the best place to remedy himself of Johnnie Tyme - the thug that shot his cousin and thought he could come back to the neighborhood acting like all was forgiven. This young buck had the nerve to tell him he did his time by law. The law? F---- the law! The only law that mattered to him was that of the streets – an eye for an eye.

As he hastily dragged the body toward the edge of the road, the shooter glimpsed what looked like a lone car in the distance. Not wanting to be identified, he abandoned the body and faded into the night.

*   *   *

Tracy, Johnna, and Slim had just dropped Reina home after celebrating her acceptance into an out-of-state teacher's training program. With the three of them grooving to the sounds of Gerald Levert as the Silver SUV glided down the road, it was Tracy who spotted the trouble first.

"Oh my God, that was a body!" Tracy cried out as she stretched her neck to peer out the window on the passenger side of the SUV.

"Nah, it's probably just a down tree or something," Slim replied as he continued down the pitch black road. Johnna, sitting in the back seat, giggled to herself and figured that Tracy was up to her usual antics. When the SUV came to an abrupt stop, Johnna's head hit the back of the driver's seat and she suddenly realized the seriousness of the situation.

"What are you doing?" Slim cried out as he fought to move Tracy's foot off of the breaks.

"Back up. Back up!" Tracy screamed.

"Are you crazy?" Slim yelled.

"I'm telling you what I know that was a body!" Tracy shouted.

Slim reluctantly backed the SUV up the road to the spot where Tracy thought she saw the body. To their surprise, lying curled up on the edge of the road was the corpse of a young African American male. A hush filled the idling SUV as the three of them sat speechless staring out the passenger side window at the body. The man's blood stained tee-shirt, faded jean shorts, and white tennis shoes left a lasting imprint in all of their minds.

It was Slim's voice that broke the uncanny silence. "We need to get out of here!" he blurted looking nervously back and forth between his side and rear view mirrors.

*   *   *

Eda was sick and tired of being sick and tired. After working a sixty hour week at the hospital, she came home and cared for Momma, fed the kids and cleaned the house - all in that order. Ever since her elderly mother had had her stroke, Eda's life had become even more worrisome. Having suffered from paralysis in her right shoulder, Eda's mother moved in with her. Eda figured her mother's social security check would help her out a bit, but in reality it barely helped with anything. Still, Eda felt good that she was able to help the woman who had helped so many throughout the years.

"Those kids...they got stuff everywhere!" Eda mumbled as she walked in the door and switched on the light to the living room. Eda yelled almost by habit, "Leida, Jamal, Tanja, Maceo, and Keonteye get down here!"

The sound of her command echoed throughout the house as she

walked through the maze of toys, shoes, and backpacks – all belonging to the children that her daughter, Sondra, had abandoned. Eda thought back to the day when she had received the call from Social Services. The children had been fending for themselves for nearly a month on junk food and water. Without hesitation, she had ushered her grandbabies into her home. When Sondra finally materialized four months later, she was so strung out that Eda almost didn't recognize her own daughter; it broke her heart. Sondra, who had once possessed the beauty and grace of an angel, now looked like a walking zombie from one of those old black and white horror films. Trying to shake the memory from her mind, Eda made her way through the house picking up the trail of coats and shoes that littered the hallway leading to the kitchen.

"I ain't no maid!" she muttered to herself as she rolled up her sleeves and walked over to the kitchen sink to wash her hands. Lost in thought, Eda moved from the sink to the refrigerator without ever noticing Momma sitting in the little wooden chair near the back door.

"Hmmm, we know that," Momma said with slurred speech as she tried to position herself comfortably in the chair.

Eda replied with a sigh, "Hey Momma. Did you see the mess them children left? I can't believe them?"

Momma was used to this routine. Eda came home everyday and complained about the mess the children left in the house. Most of the time, Momma would just listen with a short grunt because she knew no matter how much Eda fussed that she loved those babies immensely. So on this day, Momma let Eda vent and waited patiently for just the right moment to tell her the news.

"Johnnie called," Momma said as evenly as she could.

Eda was so far into her diatribe that she only half heard Momma.

"Huh," she asked starring blankly?

Momma knew that any conversation with Eda about Johnnie had to be broached with gentleness. She also knew her grandson was getting out of jail in a week. And although he had committed a horrible crime, Johnnie was their family and he needed a place to stay. She responded a little louder this time trying her best to articulate each word clearly, "I said Johnnie called."

Trying to ignore the weary feeling in her stomach Eda asked cautiously, "Well, what he have to say?"

"Well, he said he's been paroled and he'll be home soon."

The sound of hot grease popping on the stove lulled Eda's thoughts back to the night when Johnnie, her only son, took away any joy or hope she had left for any of her children. Almost five years younger than Sondra, Johnnie managed to avoid getting strung out on dope, but still he managed to get caught up in its nasty web. As part of the M Street Crew, he had a serious clash with the Big East Boys - a clash that changed his life forever. Johnnie, the trigger man, was sentenced to twenty years in the Maryland State Penitentiary. Eda had gone to visit him only once during the eight years he served for the crime. She sometimes felt guilty about that fact, but she couldn't stand to see her son behind bars. At least that's what she told herself, but the reality of the situation was that she couldn't stand to look into the eyes of a cold-hearted killer, even if it was her son. As Eda floured the chicken and placed each piece in the frying pan, she shook her head thinking how God had pulled a quick one on her – a crackhead for a daughter and a murderer for a son. She wondered what she could have done to deserve such heartache.

*   *   *

Eda hadn't talked to Momma about the letter she had received from Johnnie. Yet, she couldn't stop thinking about it. She already knew the exact date and time when her beloved baby boy would be coming home; she had known now for months. Yet, she never mentioned it to Momma or the children. Eda knew Johnnie must have told Momma about the letter when he called, but it was no surprise to her that Momma never mentioned it. That's what Eda loved so much about her mother. She had a way of letting you know she knew something without forcing the point on you. By the time the children had come back into the house and Eda had laid them out about the mess they left in the living room, Momma had mentioned how nice it would be to have a man around the house to keep Jamal, Maceo, and Keontaye in line.   By the time Eda and the children had settled down for bed, Momma had mentioned how all the stuff in the front of the basement could be moved to the back to make room for Johnnie.   Eda had learned early in her life that it was no use trying to tangle with Momma when she had her mind set on a thing.   And although Eda had decided from the moment she had read Johnnie's letter that she would allow him to move back home with them, she was not ready to talk about it just yet.

*   *   *

On the night of Johnnie's expected arrival, Eda fixed a colossal meal with all of his favorite foods – crab cakes, potato salad, and collard greens. Eda didn't tell the children about Johnnie because she wanted to surprise them. At least that's what she told Momma, but deep inside she didn't want to risk disappointing them. Besides, she still wasn't sure how to explain his prolonged absence. So on this night, Eda fixed a meal for a king and waited for the return of her prodigal son.   She asked God to give her the right words to say, but she never had the opportunity to say anything because Johnnie never came home.

*   *   *

It was the day after Reina's return trip from California and she had arranged to meet up with her friends at Lolita's to get the scoop about the body they had found on the night of her going away party. As the four of them sat hunched in a corner booth, Reina was bubbling with questions.

"So what did he have on? Oh my God, do you think the killer was still there when you pulled up?" Reina asked through swigs of lemonade.

Johnna, Tracy, and Slim looked at each other and sighed in unison. Tracy replied first.

"Well, we drove past and I thought I saw something. I screamed for Slim to stop the truck," she said.

"Yeah," Slim responded. "We backed up, saw this guy lying dead on the side of the ride, and we jetted. I drove straight to that police station on the other side of the park to report the body."

"And can you believe the police held us at the station for almost an hour asking us questions?" Johnna replied before taking a bite of her sandwich.

"And the sad part is," Tracy said as she sipped her iced tea, "that we never saw anything in the newspaper or on television about that body; it was just like he didn't exist - just another Baltimore statistic."

Reina looked down at her cheese steak and thought aloud, "Yeah, but to somebody he was a son, a brother, maybe even a father. I wonder if anyone even knows he is dead."

"That fool that shot him knows," Slim said popping a French fry into his mouth.

The three of them glared at Slim and shook their heads in laughter.

*   *   *

When Eda got home on this night, her grandbabies had surprised her by cleaning up the living room and the entire downstairs. The children and Momma were in the kitchen fixing hot dogs and baked beans as Eda sat down at the kitchen table. Her eyes asked Momma the question that her heart didn't have the courage to voice.

"No baby, he didn't call," Momma said quietly.

Eda's eyes shifted down to the floor as she replied, "I just don't know what happened to that boy. Maybe while he's running around out there, he'll catch up with that sister of his and they'll both find their way home, one day."

It was Momma this time who seemed to be the one lost in thought as she replied in what was almost a whisper, "one day."

Could of, Should of

Could of turned His back on me,
Should of turned His back on me.

Could of turned a deaf ear to me,
Should of turned a deaf ear to me.

Could of left me alone,
Should of left me alone.

Could of given up on me,
Should of given up on me.

Could of left me to die,
Should of left me to die.

Could of left me without hope,
Should of left me without hope.

Could of blocked His mercy and grace,
Should of blocked His mercy and grace.

Could of condemned my soul to hell,
Should of condemned my soul to hell.

Could of deemed me unworthy of His love,
Should of deemed me unworthy of His love.

Could of left me to die,
Should of left me to die,
But GOD gave me eternal life!

He sticks with me through thick and thin,
Hears my cries and listens more intently than a friend.
He never leaves me.
My God is always near!

He has faith in me when I doubt myself.
He loves me into wholeness and renews my heart and soul.
He prepares me for a new life in Him.
He equips me with a mighty sword that gives me power, strength, and joy.
He forgives me when it is hard to forgive myself.
He blesses me even though I am unworthy of His blessings.
He gave me His son, Jesus Christ.
He gave me salvation, deliverance, and freedom.

He should of
and he could of
But God!

Psalms of the Daughter

Psalm 1:

Hope springs eternal.
It is through hope that we will change ourselves and our neighborhoods.

It is through the hope of our children, brothers, sisters, fathers, mothers, husbands, wives, grandfathers, and grandmothers that our cities will flourish in economic rejuvenation and social solidarity.

It is through the hope of a child that the heart of man will be changed.
For change to occur, hope must spring eternal.

Psalm 2:

A Daughter's Cry.

"Love is...what?
Giving in, realizing that there are others,
Sacrificing what you believe is right
For what you feel will make things right?

Love is...what?
Waiting for something that has no name,
That does not exist except on TV
Or in my mind...in my own reality,
In my dreams or in my warped sense of affection?

Love is...what?
Making love, having sex, doing the do, boning it, laying the pipe,
Making out, getting laid, f-----, going all the way,
Getting my jones on?

Love is...what?
Taking a risk...knowing that I am putting my feelings on the line for
Someone who might not be able to do the same for me?

Love is...what?

That funny feeling inside my stomach,
A physical emotion, a mental or psychic connection,
A crossing of two souls, a mirroring of two minds,
A one night stand, a lifetime of memories?

Love is...what?
What I thought I was in,
What I think I am in,
What I want to be in?

Love is...what?
Loving you more than I love myself,
Valuing you more than me,
Putting your needs before my own?

Love is...what?
The sun rising, the morning glory,
The earth moving,
a shimmering mountaintop,
A fallen star?

Love is...what?
Hard, difficult, overbearing,
Tight, smoldering, competitive,
Cold, aching, dangerous?

Love is...what?
Warm, gentle, kind, caring,
Soft, bubbly, quiet, loud?

Love is...what?
What?"

A Biblical Response.

"If I speak with human eloquence
And angelic ecstasy but don't love,
I'm nothing but the creaking of a rusty gate.
If I speak God's Word with power,

Revealing all his mysteries
And making everything plain as day,
And if I have faith that says to a mountain,
'Jump,' and it jumps,
But I don't love, I'm nothing.
If I give everything I own to the poor
And even go to the stake to be burned as a martyr,
But I don't love, I've gotten nowhere.
So no matter what I say,

What I believe,
And what I do,
I'm bankrupt without love.

Love never gives up.
Love cares more for others than for self.
Love doesn't want what it doesn't have.
Love doesn't strut,
Doesn't have a swelled head,
Doesn't force itself on others,
Isn't always 'me first,'
Doesn't fly off the handle,
Doesn't keep score of the sins of others,
Doesn't revel when others grovel,
Takes pleasure in the flowering of truth,
Puts up with anything,
Trusts God always,
Always looks for the best,
Never looks back,
But keeps going to the end.
Love never dies...

We don't yet see things clearly,
We're squinting in a fog,
Peering through a mist.
But it won't be long before the weather clears
And the sun shines bright!

We'll see it all then,

See it all as clearly as God sees us,
Knowing Him directly just as He knows us!
But for right now, until that completeness,
We have three things to do to lead us toward that consummation:
Trust steadily in God,
Hope unswervingly,
Love extravagantly.
And the best of these three is love"

Psalm 3:

What's your habit?
Is it alcohol or food?
Gossip or Lies?
Cocaine or crack?
Heroin or Sex?
Cigarettes?
Pornography?

What's your habit - the source of your addictions?

Each one impacts us differently,
But the outcome is always the same.
We lose sight of our life goals.
We become unbalanced and disconnected.
We move away from our life center with an
overabundance or more like an over indulgence in a thing.
We experience the inability to stay atop of our life direction.
We exhibit a lack of concern for ourselves and those who depend on us
because we care more for that thing that we are trying to indulge.
We risk our safety and the safety of those we love to satisfy the longing.
The hunger of our addiction fuels our thirst for chaos.

Take a closer look and see that we all have habits that unfortunately either
knowingly or unknowingly cause havoc in our lives.
What's your habit?
What's your addiction?
Whatever it is,
like any other problem left ignored,

it will grow bigger until it nags and tears at your soul,
at your inner core until you die feeding it or die fighting it.
Only you can make the choice to break that habit!

Psalm 4:

Let Go
        And
                Let God!
Life has its ups and downs,
        Ins and outs,
                Scrapes and scratches.
        At what level do you stop blaming others for life's complications?
                At what level do you forgive and move on?
                        Can you ever forgive the unforgiveable?
                                Can you move on?
Let Go
        And
                Let God!
But these are words that are easier said than done.
        How easy is it to forgive someone who had the power to shape you,
                your inner being and your inner most thoughts?

The frustration, the anger, and the bitterness never seem to go away.
        Feelings of hurt and pain continue to tear at your heart –
                breaking it into hardened pieces of stone
                        that make you unable to forgive
                                or functionally love anyone
                                        or to functionally love yourself.
But you must let go
        And let God move in your life!
                You must fight to release the anger,
                        the pain, the bitterness,
                                and the hurt.
You must forgive the people and circumstances
        that you know did you wrong.

You must forgive and release the past which you cannot change
        because your existence,

Your future...the continuation of your life...
depends on it...
Let Go and Let God!

Psalm 5:

At what point do you give in to your inability to keep track?
You remember your life's goals and dreams of long ago.
You remember your enthusiasm to see them through.

But at what point do you throw in the towel?
At what point do you stop trying to be all you can be because you
understand that you will never be more than you are?

At what point do you stop seeking opportunities, chances and support?
At what point do you give in to the demons of desire,
lust, greed, materialism?

At what point do you stop feeling like you are even worthy to exist?
At what point does your life become a daily chore?
At what point?

God give me the strength to overcome my weaknesses.
Give me the will to live and the courage to triumph.
Keep me humble and alive with your spirit.
Set a fire in my heart and mind that will blaze
a new course of direction in my life!

Psalm 6:

My spirit is heavy,
Filled with nothingness,
Emptiness – a large hollow space.
Tears flow!

Cleanse my spirit, Lord!
Release the sorrow and sadness from my swelling heart.

Make me a new woman in Christ!

Lord, help me see in myself more than a reason but a need
to live guided by your Holy Spirit.

Psalm 7:

How many times will I continue to give my love to one
who does not wish to be loved in return?
How many times must I get hurt before I realize
that I cannot find happiness in anyone but you?
How many times, Lord?

How many times will I allow my temple to be used, abused, and disgraced?
How many times will I move forward without waiting for guidance from you?
How many times will I look for love in all the wrong places?

How many times will I sacrifice what is right for what makes me feel good?
How many times will I lose myself in search of someone other than you?
How many times will I accept less than what you have prepared for me?
How many times, Lord?
How many times?

Psalm 8:

Keep me focused, Lord
For I am being pulled in two directions.
The imbalance in my life is taking over my soul.
It is confusing my everyday thoughts,
confounding my actions, and
bringing forth utter chaos in my life.

Lord, help me through this.
Guide me on a path that is connected to you.
Keep me focused and on course!

Psalm 9:

Death lurking...
whisperings...
hushed commands...

How does it feel to know that death is lurking?
How does it feel to know that your days are numbered?
Waiting...anxiously...deteriorating...slowly.

Lord, protect me. Let your Holy Spirit be a fence around me.

Psalm 10:

I want so much to be so many things to so many people that sometimes
I forget what I am supposed to be to myself.

I act according to what I think or assume others will expect or desire of me
instead of acting in accordance to Your will.

Lord, help me to put things in the right perspective.
Help me to see that it is only You that I should strive to please.

Psalm 11:

One hundred degrees of sanity is what I am aiming for...
Ninety-nine degrees of madness is what it seems I am working toward...
Being myself outside myself...
experiencing mental anguish...
having not come full circle...
feeling unbalanced...
operating outside of my life's center...
struggling with self-hatred and oppression...
fighting discrimination and racism...
dodging the arrows of insecurity...
uncertain...
hopeless...
lost...
bitter...
angry...
frustrated...
giving into busted dreams and shattered promises.

Lord, God...right the vision for my life and make it plain!

Psalm 12:

Thank you Lord for this day!
You know the enemy tried to have his way.
Fear, doubt, mistrust, and dis-ease
all tried to make me grieve,
be depressed,
and full of unease.

I thank you for planting your Word in me!
I thank you for helping me to see
that no weapon formed against me will ever prosper.
I thank you for helping me to see
that you are my helper, my provider,
and You, Lord, are so very faithful to me.

You are Alpha and the Omega,
the Lord God Almighty,
Jehovah- Sabboath,
Jehovah-Mekoddishkem,
El Elyon,
Jehovah-Shammah,
the Victorious One!

Thank you Lord for this day!
Thank you Lord for having your way
in my life,
in my home,
on my job,
and in all things surrounding me.
I thank you, Lord, for always yielding a way.

CHAPTER TWO
RELEASE

"But for you who revere my name, the sun of righteousness will rise with healing in its wings. And you will go out and leap like calves released from the stall..."
- Malachi 4:2 (NIV)

Untitled

#1

Yesterday I died a hundred times over...
still images of that instant replay hover in my mind.
I try to turn away from the sight in front of me only to realize
I have become part of the scene...
a silhouette of anxiety, insecurity, and old pain.

Oh Lord, let your Holy Spirit fall fresh on me.
Let your love, grace, and mercy surround me, protect me, and uplift me.
Release the peace of your Holy Spirit in my life. Amen.

#2

Oh God, I thank you for being Lord over my life.
I have made so many bad decisions and choices that at times I feel utterly overwhelmed. I know that it is for your grace and mercy that I am still alive.
I thank you Lord, for my life.
I thank you for your love.
I thank you for liberty.
I ask that you help me stay focused on your Word.
Give me wisdom and discernment to make good decisions.
Lord God, give me a right spirit.
Touch my heart, my mind, and my soul.
Lord, take away anything in my life that is unpleasing to you.
And Lord, in all your infinite wisdom if you choose not to take those things away, help me to die to those things that are unlike you.
Help me to live a life that honors your Word and name! Amen.

#3

I asked for wisdom. Yet, I'm uncertain if I am able to receive it.
I don't know if I am able to face whatever it is that is God's will for my life
I asked for clarity, but I am unsure if I can handle it.

Equip me, Lord! Give me the strength I need, but most importantly give me the courage to receive your message, interpret your Word, and accept Your will for my life. Amen.

Lessons Learned

I am learning when to push and when to stand still.
I am learning the value of discernment.
I am learning that some battles aren't worth fighting.

I am learning how to work with difficult people.
I am learning how to view situations with an asset-based lens.

I am learning to see situations outside of my own reality
and to take each day as it comes.

I am learning to stand firm in my convictions
but open to other people's concerns.

I am learning to live and enjoy life in a way that pleases God.
I am learning to be accountable for my actions
and to accept responsibility for my inaction.

I am learning to esteem prayer
and to cherish its power.

I am learning to love and appreciate the people
and circumstances that God placed in my life.

I am learning the value of laughter,
and I am learning how to laugh at myself.

I am learning the art of listening.
But most importantly, I'm learning...
that I still have so much more to learn.

Acts

Kayla knew she was on the verge of doing something that she would regret. As she stood at the edge of the icy bridge rail, she tried to reason herself back to sanity.   And with the February wind slicing her face, she shivered in utter fear at what she was about to do.

*   *   *

Jay Colbert loved everything about winter. He loved the feel of the wind. He loved the chill of the night and he especially liked the fact that his shifts were longer this time of the year; it meant more money in overtime pay. He was thankful that he was even alive to appreciate it all. At one point in his life, Jay believed he would never live to see twenty-five, let alone thirty-seven. He felt blessed beyond belief to have overcome the drugs, the handful of bank robberies, his short-lived career as a hustler, and the loss of his mother to an unexpected but predictable heroin overdose. And with a life that read like an episode from *The Wire*, Jay was determined to make a clean break of his past.

A high school graduate, Jay had never gone further than a year in college. It wasn't that he lacked intelligence; he just lost interest in life. He wished now that he had obtained his Bachelor's degree instead of graduating from the Certified School of Hard Knocks. One thing he knew for sure, though, was that his life had drastically changed after meeting Rev. Parker and the brothers from Jesus Saves Ministry. It was their encouragement and support that helped Jay chart out a new direction for his life.

Pastor Parker, a big burly man with broad shoulders, saw something in Jay that no one else had ever taken the time to see. When everyone had decided that he was a lost cause, Pastor Parker refused to give up on him. His prayers, talks, encouragement and financial support had provided Jay with the guidance he needed to steer his life into a more positive direction. As a matter of fact, it was Pastor Parker who had called in a favor to one of his frat brothers and had gotten Jay his current position at the Safe Armored Truck Company. He glanced quickly in his rearview mirror at his uniform neatly pressed and hanging in the back of the truck. He chuckled to himself. Who would have thought that he of all people would end up of guarding money instead of...well, he had to laugh at that one. God did work in mysterious ways.

*   *   *

Gripping the steering wheel, Jay rested his head against the leather headrest of his Escalade. Like a sleek, black cougar, he silently moved down the boulevard, but unlike that animal, he was not in search of prey. Jay was heading home from a long night's work just having completed a thirteen-hour shift. Jay looked at the clock on his dashboard; it was half past midnight. He cherished this time of night or rather morning. It was the only time he could drive down the boulevard in peace without the howl of angry car horns or the roar of rumbling trucks. As Jay crossed the Harriet Tubman Bridge, he slowed down a notch to view the river front. It was an impressive sight to see, but on this night something else caught his attention. Jay stopped the Escalade in the emergency lane and leaned over his steering wheel to get a better view; he was unprepared for the sight before him.

*   *   *

Kayla – too engrossed in her nightmare to notice anyone else – wavered a few minutes before stepping off the bridge rail. Within seconds, two strong arms hauled her back to safety. With one arm wrapped around Kayla's neck and the other wrapped around her torso, Jay lifted her off the bridge rail in what seemed like lightening speed. Instinctively, he turned their bodies opposite the bridge railing and held onto Kayla as if she might take another leap forward toward the icy blackness below.

"What are you doing?" he shouted over the whistling wind.

Kayla with tears streaming down her face struggled to escape the stranger's grasp. "Let me go," she said breathlessly. "Why can't you just let me die?" Kayla moaned almost to the ground as she tried to wiggle free from Jay's embrace.

"Stop fighting me!" he screamed.

Towering over her, Jay tightened his grip around Kayla. As he tilted his head toward hers, he whispered words of comfort into her ear. Slowly, Kayla's body started to sag as she succumbed to the calm of his words.

"Freeze!"

The screams of the police officers took them both by surprise. Jay looked up to see two uniformed officers with guns pointing directly at him.

"Hey, man. It's not what it looks like!" he tried to yell above the wind.

"Shut up and let the lady, go!" one of the officers shouted.

"O.k., I'm unarmed," Jay said as he released his hold on Kayla.

Another officer rushed over to Kayla and pulled her to the other side of the bridge. Instinctively, Jay reached into his coat pocket to get his wallet and I.D. He never heard the shots that pierced the night air.

As Jay fell backward, it seemed all time stopped. Only the shrill sound of Kayla's scream brought everyone back to the reality that was before them: Jay lying on the ground with blood running from - seemingly - everywhere.

Kayla watched in numb horror. She didn't recognize her own voice as she cried out, "You shot him. Oh my God, you shot him!"

The officer, unmoved by Kayla's cries or the sight of the man he had just shot, looked at Kayla with disgust. "Lady, give me a break! He was trying to hurt you. I did you a favor."

The tears began to flow down Kayla's face again as she sobbed, "No! No! Oh my God! Oh, my God...No! He was trying to help me!" She looked down at Jay's bullet-ridden body, then over to the bridge rail, and whispered to no one in particular, "He was trying to stop me from jumping."

Both officers followed her gaze from the almost lifeless body of the man before them to the bridge rail. Only one ran back to his cruiser and radioed for help.

Kayla wasn't a praying woman. She had never really believed that

God cared much about her. Sometimes she wondered even if there was a God. Yet on this brisk February night, she prayed for the first time in her life for a man she didn't even know.

*   *   *

Kayla had become a frequent visitor at the hospital ever since the night of the shooting. She still couldn't believe a total stranger had risked his life to save hers. As she stood alongside his hospital bed, she studied the man's face - trying to discern the motive behind his courageous act. With a heavy heart, Kayla sighed and walked over to the window. As she sat down on the windowsill, her thoughts turned away from the unconscious man stretched out before her and onto the circumstances which had led to her unthinkable act.

*   *   *

With a new job in a new city, it had at first felt to Kayla that she was on top of the world and was finally in control of the craziness that had always been her life. Yet, in the months that followed, her life had spiraled into a coil of confusion. She couldn't pinpoint when she had started losing control. Maybe it was the monotony of getting up everyday and going home to an empty apartment. She hated being alone. Yet even when she was in the presence of others, she felt like an outsider. No matter what she did she couldn't seem to shake the emptiness. She had tried clubbing to surround herself with people and music hoping to keep her mind off the loneliness. She had tried drinking to numb the pain. She had slept with more people than she cared to remember trying to clasp that feeling - that moment of utter ecstasy when it felt like she was in complete control. Yet with each of her bad decisions, Kayla realized what little self-control she actually had. Nothing – no matter how outrageous – seemed to numb the ache of her heart. Her day-to-day activities and her humdrum life were all glimpses of memories that she wanted desperately to end.

Sitting on the windowsill, Kayla looked at the machines and tubes connected to Jay; she felt a sense of obligation to him. She had accompanied him in the ambulance on the night he was shot and had been standing vigil at his bedside ever since. Kayla had learned her mystery hero's name and occupation from the television reporters. She learned everything else about him from Pastor Parker who startled her during one of her crying spells that first night she had visited the hospital. Pastor Parker had stood at the doorway and watched her for nearly an hour before Kayla realized she and her mystery hero had company.

* * *

Pastor Parker had known who she was the minute he had entered the room. He had watched the news reports and read the countless news articles. He had even served as Jay's official family spokesperson demanding justice from the Tubman City Police Force who wanted to disregard the fact that two of their officers had gunned down an unarmed man – one that had no less just saved a delirious woman from jumping to her death off of a one-hundred and thirty-five foot bridge. Pastor Parker knew that if Kayla had not witnessed the entire charade, the officers probably would have fabricated an incident to cover their blunder. He also knew that she was the reason this had all happened in the first place. He had known the first time he saw Kayla that she was a lost soul and had begun that first day talking to her about the love of Jesus Christ. They talked well into the night and when Mrs. Parker stopped in to see Jay it seemed she picked up right where the Pastor had left off. All Kayla could do was cry. The tears just wouldn't stop. She cried for herself, but most of all she cried for the pain she had caused Jay. Just when it seemed that she had run out of tears, Mrs. Parker eased the little book in her hand and asked her to begin reading.

"The Book of Psalms?" asked Kayla.

"Yup, and you can begin at Psalm One," Mrs. Parker replied.

Kayla glanced down at the little book as she thumbed through the pages and looked back up at Mrs. Parker with her eyebrows raised. "But there are a hundred-and-fifty of them," Kayla said.

"And your point is what?" Mrs. Parker replied with a glint of a smile that faded when she turned back to look at Jay lying under the stark white sheets of the hospital bed. "Based on Dr. Hudson's report, it's no telling how long Jay will be in this coma. The Book of Psalms was his favorite book of the Bible. Start with this one right here," Mrs. Parker said as she reached over and opened the little book in Kayla's hand.

Pastor Parker stood up and put a firm hand on Kayla's shoulder.

"Read it aloud," he said just before leaving the room.

Mrs. Parker also encouraged Kayla to read aloud. She told her it would help to soothe her restlessness. So it was forty-two days ago that Kayla had begun reading aloud each Psalm one by one. When Kayla got to Psalm Six that first week something clicked inside of her.

"The Lord heard my supplication; the Lord will receive my prayer."

Kayla recognized the agony in the writer's words and her heart softened just enough for the healing to begin. A few weeks later at Psalm Eighteen, Kayla made a declaration from her heart.

"I will love you, Lord. Oh, Lord, my strength. You are my rock, my fortress, my deliverer, my God, my strength in you I will trust. You are my protection, the horn of my salvation, my righteousness."

When Kayla reached Psalm Twenty-three, the tears gushed like waves from her eyes as she recognized the scripture and grasped the true meaning of the words she had heard this stranger whisper in her ear that dreadful night.

"The Lord is my shepherd; I shall not be in want. He makes me to lie down in green pastures; he leads me beside still waters. He restores my soul. He guides me in paths of righteousness for His name's sake. Even though, I walk through the valley of the shadow of death. I will fear no evil, for you are with me; your rod and your staff they comfort me. You prepare a table before me in the presence of my enemies. You anoint my head with oil; my cup overflows. Surely goodness and love will follow me all the days of my life, and I will dwell in the house of the Lord, forever."

On that day in the hospital room, Kayla opened her heart to God and accepted Jesus as her personal Savior. With the drip of Jay's I.V. and the other sounds of the hospital room weaving in with her thoughts, she told God about her pain, her longing, and her need for release. She asked Him for forgiveness; and for the first time in Kayla's life, she felt a sense of peace.

*   *   *

Six weeks later, Jay awoke from the coma. He didn't recognize his surroundings, but he could hear beeps and distant voices. When he tried to move, the pain was excruciating. Yet even through the throbbing, he was able to focus on what sounded like a woman reading Psalm 42.

"As the deer pants for streams of water, so my soul pants for you, O God. My soul thirsts for God, for the living God. When can I go and meet with God? My tears have been my food day and night, while men say to me all day long, 'Where is your God?' These things I remember as I pour out my soul: how I used to go with the multitude, leading the procession to the house of God, with shouts of joy and thanksgiving among the festive throng. Why are you downcast, O my soul? Why so disturbed within me? Put your..."

With his eyes still shut, Jay groaned as he tried to reach in the direction of the woman's voice. Startled, Kayla stopped in mid-sentence and looked in alarm at Jay. By the time he had managed to open his eyes, Kayla had already rushed out of the room to find his nurse. The hallway soon bustled with the hurried footsteps of doctors and nurses - rushing in and out to check on the hero.

"Mr. Colbert, my name is Dr. Hudson. You are a lucky man. Four bullets entered your chest and missed your heart by two centimeters each. Fortunately, we were able to remove them all during surgery."

Jay managed to mumble, "Blessed."

"Blessed, young man is what I would say you are," Dr. Hudson said as he turned to give directions to Jay's nurse and headed toward the door. As Dr. Hudson made his way into the hallway, he gave Kayla an encouraging nod alerting her that it was alright to go back into Jay's room.

Kayla stood frozen in the hallway trying to find the courage to face the stranger who had saved her life. She struggled with the guilt she felt in putting this man in harm's way. A sense of dread surged from the pit of Kayla's stomach as she let out a long sigh and leaned back against the wall. Remembering Mrs. Parker's advice to pray whenever she felt overwhelmed with anxiety or fear, Kayla closed her eyes, raised her hands, and lifted a silent prayer to God.

* * *

Pastor Parker and Mrs. Parker were en-route to the hospital when they received the urgent call from Jay's doctor. As they stepped off the elevator, they both had the same reaction at the sight of Kayla praying in the hallway. Pastor Parker and Mrs. Parker walked over to Kayla and gently took her hands into their own. She looked up and gave them a weary nod. As if he could see into her soul, Pastor Parker stared deep into Kayla's tear soaked eyes. He gave her a reassuring nod and uttered a heart-felt prayer.

"Dear God, we thank you for your love and mercy. God, we thank you for your grace. We thank you for giving us your son, Jesus Christ who died on the cross for our sins. Lord, we don't always understand the cards that you deal us in life. Yet, we trust that your perfect will be done. Lord, we thank you for watching over Jay. We thank you for sparing his life. Lord, we know that he is your vessel and we thank you for saving him. We thank you for using him to bring one of your daughters back home to you. Lord, we are so thankful for Kayla. We thank you for sparing her life, and we thank you for her new found faith in you. We ask that you continue to guide and protect both Kayla and Jay. Be with them, for the days ahead will be even more difficult than those behind. Encourage their hearts and keep them firm in you. Let your will be done in their lives. We pray these things in the name of Jesus, Amen."

When Pastor Parker finished the prayer, there wasn't a dry eye between the three of them. Jay, in his room, couldn't help but overhear the familiar voice in the hallway. He used every bit of strength he could muster to turn his head toward the door and was a bit overwhelmed when his spiritual mother and father walked into the room with the most beautiful woman he'd ever seen. Looking back and forth between the Parkers and Kayla, Jay knew that his life once again would never be the same.

I Thought You Would Be The One

I thought you would be the one.
I thought it would be you.
I thought that everything about you was so right,
so true.

I wanted to believe that God had truly sent you.
Yet, each day I slowly recognized the mounting clues.
Still, I tried desperately to hold on...
Hoping, wanting to impress you.
I pretended I was in control...
wearing a happy face when ever you came around,
trying to say and do the right thing to capture your heart.
You see, I wanted so badly to end my journey into loneliness,
end the coldness and rid myself of the dark.

I tried to be someone that you wanted me to be,
but realized that all I needed to be was me.
The me I know is kind and sweet.
Beautiful at heart,
beyond skin deep.
But I don't think you ever glimpsed that person.
I don't think you ever really saw me.

The me you saw was filled with fear and doubt.
She let you abuse her body,
her mind,
and misuse her from the start.
She compromised what she knew was right...
for a pretense of love and warmth.
She forgot God's promise to her
as she stumbled along in the dark.

I talked to God about it.
I cried out to him for relief.
Oftentimes I ended up just crying myself to sleep.

More than once I can remember a long hard sleepless night,
the staring into the darkness before dawn's early light.
Sometimes I wondered why God made my life this way,
but soon I matured in Christ realizing that every decision I made
impacted my life in every way.

So, I asked God for forgiveness.
I asked Him to show me a new way
and He sent his angels to comfort me,
to guide me through each new day.

It still gets dark and lonely at times,
but I always see the light
because God's grace and mercy...
provides protection and covering over my life.

Jewel

Lisette Langley was nineteen years old when she had Lisa. Everyone seemed to know what she should do and gave more advice than she could handle, but Lisette prayed for guidance and knew that the little jewel in her stomach was truly a blessing from God. As the years passed, Lisette watched her daughter blossom. Things had not been easy for them. They both learned a lot about struggle, but Lisette had her faith in God and two wonderful parents who helped her raise Lisa. And when Lisa matured into adulthood, it had been hard for Lisette to let go, but in the end she had no choice.

*   *   *

It started with what Lisa thought was a cold. After three weeks of dealing with a runny nose and a sore throat, she thought she was in the clear until her body was overpowered by fever. When the fever finally broke, Lisa thought surely she had recovered, but then the yeast infections and the skin rashes picked up where it seemed the other ailments left off. Lisa was trying desperately to leave her memories of Thornton College behind, finish out a year at a new university, complete her work-study, and get over Kevin. So, she tried to deal with all the sickness as best she could and attributed most of it to the stress. With so much on her mind, Lisa had no time to find a reason for the itching, the burning, or the cold from hell. She pressed on without complaint and dealt with each blow as it came – all muffled by the pain of breaking up with Kevin.

Lisa and Kevin had been an item since high school. Everyone thought they were the perfect pair. While Lisa's Mom and Grandmother raised her with the expectation to attend college, Kevin – a year ahead of Lisa - enrolled at a local community college just to pass the time. When Lisa decided to attend Thornton College, he followed her there and although she did not survive her freshman year at Thornton, she did survive Kevin Larkin - at least almost until the end.

Throughout that first year at Thornton, Lisa felt the stress of being a thousand miles away from her Mom and Grandmother. The two of them were her foundation and strength. So after almost flunking out of her freshman year, Lisa took her sophomore year off from Thornton and returned to Maryland to clear her head. Eventually, she transferred to Tubman University which was less than an hour train ride from her hometown.

When Kevin had first learned of Lisa's decision to transfer, he was totally against it. He argued that he was all the support she needed. Amidst the stress of classes, work-study, and exams, Lisa had less and less patience for her waning relationship with Kevin. And although she reassured him that the transfer to Tubman would not mean an end to their relationship, she knew deep in her heart that their time had come to an end. He had not only lied about his sexuality, but he strung her along in his web of lies. Even after learning of his deception, Lisa still hoped that she would be able to win his love. She was crazy about Kevin. She remembered the first time she opened up to her Mom about the relationship.

"What do you mean it just kind of happened?" her mother asked. "You trying to tell me you all just magically ended up in bed together?"

Lisa rolled her eyes and switched the receiver to her other ear. "No, Ma. You know what I mean. We started out studying in my room. Then, we ordered some pizza. I showed him my CD collection. We started to groove, and next thing I knew we were at it."

"Well, it sure sounds planned to me. He knew what he was doing."

Lisa smiled and replied, "Yeah, he sure did!"

"Lisa Laray Langley, don't you get fresh with me. I thought I taught you better than this. Don't you know if you don't value yourself enough to hold out then the one you are giving it up to will not see any value in you? Lord, what am I going to do with this child? Tell me you all at least used a condom," snapped Lisette.

For the first time since the start of the phone call, silence had entered the conversation.

"Ahhhhhh, Lisa."

"I know Ma, but you act like I'm sleeping with the whole world. He was my first, and he is going to be my last. Plus, I'm on the pill. And you know Kevin is not the type to play the field."

"Look-a-here, girl. I don't care what type he is and you better not be sleeping with the whole world. As a matter of fact, I am not too keen on you sleeping with Kevin, but that's another subject for discussion. Anyway, I do expect you to use that pretty head that God gave you. Getting pregnant is the least of your worries. Pills won't protect you from a sexually transmitted disease."

"Mommy! Why do you always have to go through this with me about Kevin? You make Kevin out to be a dog. He loves me and wouldn't do anything to hurt me."

"Baby girl, love ain't got nothing to do with it. Kevin is a man. Now, I'm not saying all men cheat, but what I am saying is that men will be men. When you been in this world long as me you realize that sometimes things don't happen the way you plan them and sometimes people hurt you even without trying."

*   *   *

After working overtime for a year, Lisa had saved enough money to put a down payment on her first semester at Tubman University. Just as she was beginning to get into the swing of things, her body collapsed under what she thought was a bad cold. Lisa was vomiting and feverish for nearly a week. Her new roommate concerned about Lisa's deteriorating health finally broke down and phoned Lisette. Lisette was able to encourage her daughter through worried telephone calls to visit the infirmary, and she arranged for Lisa to see the family doctor on her next holiday break.

Lisa stepped off the train at Penn Station and was bombarded by the crowds of people at the station meeting up with loved ones and friends for the Thanksgiving holiday weekend. Although she still felt sick, the sight of her Mom and Grandmother brought an instant smile to her face.

"Baby girl, you lost so much weight," Lisette said worriedly.

Lisa glanced at her mother and then her grandmother. She turned to embrace her grandmother and said jokingly, "Hey Grandma that smile on your face tells me that at least you're happy to see me."

Lisa's grandmother just stood there smiling back at her. She was so proud of her grandbaby. That girl was the first one in the family to attend college. She pulled Lisa toward her and said, "Baby, don't you pay your mother any mind. Come on over here and give me some love!"

As Lisa hugged her grandmother, she reached over and pulled her mother into the embrace.

*   *   *

It was nearly a month after the train station reunion, when Lisette received the covert call from the family's physician.

"Charles, are you sure? You all ran so many tests...maybe you mixed one up by mistake," Lisette said anxiously. She could only listen in shock while her brother assured her of Lisa's diagnosis. Lisette felt numb and almost dropped the receiver. She barely managed to whisper, "Charles you have been Lisa's physician since she was in my womb. I thank you for sharing this with me first, but Lisa is an adult and you need to tell her. No, I think it should come from you. Yes, of course I'm going to be there for her. I just want to give her some time to sort this out for herself."

*   *   *

It took Lisa almost six months to finally confide in her Mom that she had AIDS. She first confided in her childhood friend, Tiesha. Tiesha being the good friend she was accompanied Lisa to every AIDS seminar, support group, and education class they could find hoping to learn more about the disease. It was Tiesha who kept urging Lisa to tell her mother and grandmother.

"You need to tell them," Tiesha said quietly as she sat next to Lisa.

"I can't," sobbed Lisa, "She will be so disappointed in me. Everyone will be so disappointed in me. And she probably already knows, anyway.

I'm sure Uncle Charles told her."

"Oh Lisa, come on, you don't know that for sure. And anyway, you need your Mom and Grandma now more than ever. Girl, this is serious. Your new doctor has you on this crazy cocktail of drugs, you are going through a major case of depression, and in case you haven't noticed you are scaring me to death," Tiesha screamed.

"Why don't you just leave me alone? Lisa shouted.

Tears swelled in Tiesha's eyes but her voice held steady as she reached over to touch Lisa's shoulder. "You can say anything you like to me. I understand that you are hurt and angry at the world right now. But I am not leaving you alone and if you won't tell your mother then I will. Lisa, you have so many people who love you. You do not have to take this on alone!"

Lisa looked away shaking her head. "What will they think? Everyone will talk about me. Everyone will whisper, 'you know she got the bug'."

"Girl, who cares what they think and who cares if they talk about you. If you recall, they did more than talk about Jesus Christ. The only person you owe an explanation to is God. Please pray about this Lisa. It's not too late for you to accept Jesus into your life. His love will see you through! Give me your hand I want to pray with you."

Tiesha grabbed Lisa's hand as tears streamed down both of their faces.

"Dear God, I thank you so much for your love. I thank you for my friend Lisa. God you know her heart and her situation. Lord, she needs you right now. We need you right now. Lord, comfort her. Help her to see that there is light in all this darkness. Lord, strengthen her. Heal her body. Surround her with your grace and mercy, Lord. Send your angels to comfort her so that she knows that you are with her always. I ask these things in the name of Jesus. Amen."

Lisa hugged Tiesha and asked her quietly, "Will you go with me when I tell Mommy?"

"Of course," Tiesha replied with a tired smile.

*   *   *

"Go ahead, Mommy, scream at me! Tell me you told me so. Just go ahead," Lisa cried. Standing before her mother, Lisa's body shook violently from the force of her tears.

Lisette looked over at Tiesha who was also crying. The sight of the pair sobbing together reminded her of how she used to whip their butts when they were young. She remembered how they always seemed to be up to something. Lisette walked over and pulled both Lisa and Tiesha to her. After giving them each a hug, she managed to say through her own tears, "Ain't no use in worrying over spilt milk, Lisa. What's done is done. You go ahead and cry. Let the tears flow. I'm right here by your side and when you are ready we will fight this together!"

And before the night was over, the three of them had cried a river of tears. Through it all, they made a pact to each other and to God to trust and believe.

*   *   *

That night almost three and a half years ago now seemed like an eternity. As Lisette sat by her daughter's hospital bed, she wiped away the tears from her own face. The past couple of months had been extremely difficult for her jewel. In addition to fighting five infections in her body, Lisa was battling a rare strain of cancer and coping with pneumonia. She had lost so much weight that she barely had enough strength to stand. It had been touch and go for nearly a month and the doctors really didn't know what to tell Lisette or Lisa. "We are doing our best," is what the doctors kept saying to her with eyes that only half looked her way before glancing at some spot on their notepads. Lisette could never understand why people hated to look directly into another person's eyes to announce bad news. All her life, she had lived through bad news and watched people look over her, through her, but never at her and this is just what these doctors were doing. Lisette knew that Lisa's fate was in God's hands, not theirs.

"Hey Mommy," Lisa said in wispy voice.

Lisette looked over at her daughter and was so thankful that Lisa could still smile. "Baby girl, how are you feeling this morning?"

"I'm fine. Tiesha stopped by last night with Jasmine and little Sean. Can you believe she and Big Sean will be celebrating their sixth anniversary next month?"

Lisette replied, "Girl, you know babies don't stay babies for long." She paused and took a really good look at her baby girl lying there so fragile and small in the oversized hospital bed. Lisette tried hard to fight back the tears as she turned her head abruptly to look out the window.

"I see you, Mommy. Stop trying to hide your tears. It's o.k. You can let it go...let it go. You have been trying so hard to be strong for me, and I want you to know how much I love and appreciate you. I want you to know that you don't have to be strong for me anymore."

Lisette just couldn't hold it in any longer. Her sobs came in long wails as she laid her head against Lisa's hospital bed.

Lisa sighed. Reaching over to stroke her mother's hair, she took the role of the comforter. "It's okay, Mommy. I'm feeling so much better. Do you know I'm going home tomorrow?"

Lisette wiped the tears from her eyes and looked up at Lisa. "Did the doctors tell you that?" Lisette asked.

Lisa didn't respond to her mother's question. She just turned her head toward the hospital window and smiled. "Don't worry," Lisa said softly. "Go home and get some rest." She turned slowly toward her mother and quipped with a tired giggle, "You've been here all week. Look at you, I'm sorry to say but you look a mess! Maybe you should be in that bed next to me."

Lisette looked at her child lying in the hospital bed and smiled. In all her pain, Lisa was trying to laugh and make her feel better. She couldn't have asked for a more beautiful daughter.

*   *   *

The next morning Lisette decided to skip work to take a surprise to her jewel. She knew that Lisa loved chocolate cake, and Lisette awoke early that morning determined to bake one for her. After whipping up a chocolate prize that put her other cakes to shame, Lisette rushed into the bathroom to shower and dress. She couldn't wait to share this tasty delight with Lisa. When Lisette arrived at the hospital, it was as busy as usual. The corridors were filled with the chaos of doctors, nurses, patients, and visitors all hurrying back and forth to their destinations. Lisette had become strangely familiar with this scenario. She walked hurriedly toward the elevator trying to balance the cake in her hands. When the doors opened onto Lisa's floor, the head nurse was standing guard at the nurse's station.

"Ms. Langley, thank goodness you are here. We just tried phoning your job," the head nurse said exasperatedly as she walked hastily toward Lisette.

"Well, I thought I would stop by and bring a special treat for Lisa," Lisette said as she tried to keep the cake upright in her hands.

The head nurse sighed. She knew that there was no easy way of saying it, so she said it as gently as she could. "Ms. Langley, we lost Lisa a few minutes ago. I am so sorry. I told the other nurses to keep her in the room until we could locate you."

Lisette, who was still struggling to steady the cake in her hand while walking in vivacious strides, came to an immediate halt in front of the doorway leading to Lisa's room.

Would you like for me to go inside with you?" the head nurse whispered.

Lisette turned slightly and looked directly into the nurse's eyes; she didn't avoid Lisette's gaze. She continued to look worriedly at her. Overwhelmed with grief, Lisette dropped the cake and collapsed onto the floor. "I don't understand," she sobbed. "It seemed like she was doing so much better. She even told me last night that she was going home today."

The head nurse rushed over to help Lisette.

"Ms. Langley, you know that this is an extremely complicated disease. At this stage, it is really tricky. Sometimes just as patients seem to be getting better, we lose them. I can't explain it. All I know is that God takes care of all of His children, and your daughter was one of God's own. I'm so sorry for your loss. Is there anyone I can call?"

As if talking to the air, Lisette responded, "Please call my parents."

*　　　*　　　*

Several months had passed since the funeral and Lisette's world was still in a blur. She awakened one morning to the chirping of birds and bright rays of sunshine. As Lisette set-up on the side of the bed to take in the beauty of this spring morning, she decided it would be a great day to work in the flower garden that she and Lisa had created a few years back. This year, Lisette was set on adding some Gardenias around the pathway leading to the patio. Instinctively, she reached for the phone to call Lisa. Her hand brushed the pink booklet on her night table. Lisette looked down and recognized the program from Lisa's Home-going Ceremony. It jostled her back to reality; she had lost her jewel. Lisette's only consolation was that she knew Lisa was at rest in the arms of the Lord.

Liberation Letter #1

Dear Men of My Life,

I have decided to loose you from my mind, my heart, and my space. I am tired of sleeping with your shifting spirits and making love to your empty vessels. So today, I have come to the decision that I will release each and every one of you to make room for my complete healing and purification. You see, I refuse to be a dumping ground for someone else's trash or for someone who would treat me like trash. I forgive myself for loving you, and I forgive you for not knowing how to love me. I pray the best for you.

I have traded my baggage for dancing shoes, and I am dancing to the drum beat that is my life. And with lifted hands, I am dancing with a joyful spirit and a Queen's heart as I wait in great expectation for the man/King God has ordained for me.

> Goodbye and God Bless,
> God's Daughter

Hold On!

I know you are facing some serious challenges in your life,
and I want you to know that you are not alone.
I want you to know how much I love you.
And most importantly,
I want to remind you how much God loves you.

He is with you every step of the way.
So, don't despair.
Don't give up!

I want you to know that I care
and I am here for you,
if you should need a shoulder to cry on,
an ear to scream in
or a hand to hold.

So, don't give up...
Trust God and
Hold on!

This I Know

I know I am truly covered by the Blood of Jesus.
I know His angels of protection surround me.

I know my God is present even through the trials and tribulations.
I know although I sometimes feel like throwing in the towel
and waving that white flag of surrender,
God wraps His love around me.
His grace and mercy lets me know that I can not only survive another day,
but that there will be many days for me to thrive and prosper.

I know although crazy things continue to happen in my life
I am still a child (daughter) of the most High.

I know my life was paid with a cost.
I know God's spirit is alive and dwells inside of me!
But, most importantly, I know I am free!

Come Home Black Man

Come home Black man...
You who are searching for truth only to find recycled lies.

Come home Black man...
You who are struggling for release only to be burdened down by the strain of life.

Come home Black man...
You whose cynicism and doubt have bankrupt your faith.

Come home Black man...
You who are brokenhearted, disrespected, and devalued.

Come home Black man...
You who have abandoned your destiny and surrendered to an erroneous fate.

Come home to true love – pure, warm, and complete.
Come home to the everlasting gleam of divine light.
Come home to the ultimate sage and the greatest of all mysteries.
Come home to the grace of forgiveness and true liberation.

Come home Black man...
Come Home!

God is waiting patiently for your triumphant return.

CHAPTER THREE
FREEDOM

"Stand fast therefore in the liberty by which Christ has made us free, and do not be entangled again with a yoke of bondage."
- Galatians 5:1 (NKJV)

A Day in Christ

I'm driving down the street
and like a bad movie
I watch an episode of my life unfold before me.

I try to focus on the road ahead
and again another twisted scene haunts me.

I try to turn off the picture
but one memory after the other
reminds me of the careless life I've lived.
My vision becomes distorted
as my mind begins to embrace the madness.

And then, a still small voice speaks to me
and reminds me that I am His child.
I am a daughter of the Most High.
I have accepted Jesus Christ as my personal Savior
and all my sins are forgiven.

I smile shaking my head as I begin shouting praises to God.
Lips moving,
tears flowing,
and hallelujahs rising in my throat -
I drive on down that road
with the peace of God
and a new vision in my heart.

As the driver in the car next to me wonders why
that crazy woman is talking to herself!

Back In this Place Again

Lord, God, it's me again.
I'm back in this place it seems again and again.
Each time that I encounter this phase in my life,
I try to use your Word and faith to keep me connected to the light.

Last time it seemed I fell short of your grace.
The time before I know I fell flat on my face.
Before that I was just a total disgrace –
Busted, disgusted, and acting with haste.
And here I am back in this place again.

This time I walked according to your Word.
This time I fasted and studied your Word.
This time I took time to fellowship with your Saints.
This time I worshipped and prayed my way through.
Yet, here I am Lord...what should I do?
I'm back in this place once again,
But for the first time I don't feel like it's the end.
I feel like I can keep going on.
I feel your grace, giving me the strength to press on.
I don't know when and I don't know how,
But I know you will see me through somehow.

My faith in you is growing each day,
Even more clearly, your Holy Spirit is showing me the way.
I'm still in the same place as I was before,
But this time, God, I won't do as before.
I won't try to make everything all right.
I won't try to ease the pain by night.
I will trust and believe that you have this day.
I will stand and be still,
Knowing that you will make a way.

And although I am back in this place once again,
I am standing still steadfast to the end.
I am acting with faith and trusting, too.
I am standing still and waiting on you.

A Conversation with God

Woke up this morning with tears in my eyes
trying to figure out why my love has not arrived.

Recognizing that I am extremely obsessed
with finding Mr. Right and finally getting hooked,
I cried out to God asking,
"When Lord, When!"

God silently answered,
"When you become your own best friend.
When you love yourself the way you crave that others would.
When you realize that I am pleased with you.
When you take the time to cherish who you are.
When you realize that you are one of my shining stars.
When you awake in my promises with your head held high.
When you stop asking me, 'Lord, why?'
It is at that moment my Word will become flesh
And you - my daughter - will realize I have saved you for the best!"

A New Day is Coming

I'm just coming into the realization that this thing is not all about me.
I'm just starting to understand a little more each day about being set free.
Expecting the worst but praying for the best
How ridiculous is that?
Existing here and somewhere in between,
Being but not fully living,
Just surviving it seems.

Trusting myself not to those whom I love,
But in God's love alone and
Realizing that God is not just above,
But with me,
And all around me,
In me and through me.
I am His love.

Giving out more than what I take in
Making an effort to be a better friend.
Waiting and watching,
Knowing God will provide.

Excited to know that I am the product of His love.
Excited to know that there is more to this thing
More to being whole than finding the right man with a ring,
So much more to this thing called love.

And I can see me coming through,
Breaking the chains,
Busting through the pain,
And watching the dawn
As this new day
Moves me on to new aspirations.

The Woman I Am

"Dipped in chocolate, bronzed with elegance, enameled with grace, toasted with beauty, My Lord, she is a Black woman!
- Yosef Ben-Jochannan, Historian

Who am I?

I am a daughter, granddaughter, sister, niece, aunt, cousin...friend.

Who am I?

I am God's daughter, His child, and His Intercessor.

Who am I?

I am an educator, a student, and a lifelong learner.

Who am I?

I am a woman of substance learning from the mistakes of her past.

Who am I?

I am an active voter and a concerned citizen.

Who am I?

I am a resident tired of witnessing the neglect of a City and the genocide of the people within.

Who am I?

I am a Proverbs 31 woman - a precious gem.

Who am I?

I am a prayer warrior.

Who am I?

I am one person whose faith in, hope for, and love of God has pulled her through.

Who am I?

I am dipped in chocolate, bronzed with elegance, and enameled in grace.

Who am I?

I am a beautiful Black woman!

Salvation

"It seems like everyone is looking at us," Tara whispered as she reached inside her oversized Liz Claiborne bag for a pair of shades to shield her eyes from the blazing sun.

"It is only because they never saw a more beautiful couple," replied Patrick - her fiancé.

"Or maybe they are laughing at me in this ugly wheelchair," Tara sighed.

"Ah, don't be so hard on yourself. You know your doctor said there could be a possibility of you regaining your ability to walk before the year's end. That's why he referred you to that specialist in East Baltimore," Patrick reminded her.

"I know, but that appointment is two weeks from now and I wish I could do something about this now!" Tara sighed.

"Don't' worry, everything is going to be alright," he murmured as he rushed them down the path leading to Harbor East.

"Patrick, can you take it down a notch? We might get a ticket from the wheelchair police," Tara chuckled.

"Oh, don't we have jokes today?" Patrick said with an impatient smile. "Listen, I have to meet this fellow at 6 p.m. and it is almost a quarter till. Hang tight. We are almost there."

As he pushed Tara across the boardwalk, Patrick spotted his contact. He moved Tara's chair in the shade near the water's edge. "I'll see you in a few," Patrick said. And with a quick kiss on Tara's forehead, he was gone.

Tara didn't mind the wait; she loved the outdoors just as much as she loved Patrick. Ever since the day she met him, her life had not been the same. Lost in thought, Tara felt her wheelchair suddenly jerk forward. She looked around and saw the exasperation in Patrick's eyes.

"That was quick," she said hesitantly.

"Let's go," Patrick replied sharply.

"What's wrong?" she asked.

"Let's go!" grunted Patrick as he wheeled her away from the crowd of people sauntering to and fro on the boardwalk.

Tara was uneasy. She knew a sudden change in attitude like this usually meant an argument was soon to follow; she was on edge. Lately her arguments with Patrick were becoming more physical than she could bear. And frankly, she wasn't sure how much more she could handle. When they entered the condo, it started.

"It is always about you," he hollered!

Tara was caught off guard by Patrick's comment and was even less prepared for his next action. When he jerked her wheelchair around, Tara fell out of it. She hit the floor with a thud and tried to position herself into a fetal position, but her legs felt like bricks and were just too heavy for her to move.

"Get up," Patrick shouted!

Tara tried to reach for something to gain her balance as she screamed back at Patrick, "You know I can't walk. Why are you doing this to me?" Crying hysterically, she tried to maneuver herself on the floor to lean up against her wheel chair, but it kept moving backward every time she tried to grip it.

"You act so helpless, sometimes. You aren't even trying," Patrick said with a tone of disgust in his voice as he stepped over Tara who had managed to pull her upper body up into a sitting position on the floor. Exhausted from the effort, she fell back on the carpeted floor. As she laid stretched prostrate on the floor, Tara wiped the tears from her eyes and uttered a hushed prayer.

"Oh Jesus, I need you Lord. I don't know what to do. You know it

hasn't always been this way between Patrick and me. Lord, help Patrick with his temper. Help him release his anger and frustration in a healthier way. Dear God, let your Holy Spirit surround and protect me from harm's way. I'm at a loss on what to do. I need you Lord. I need your guidance. I need you to right this situation. Lord, I..."

Tara, unable to finish the prayer, wept silently. When Patrick walked back into the living room and saw her crying outstretched on the floor, he reached down and gently lifted her back into her wheelchair. Patrick kneeled down in front of Tara and apologized. He vowed never to physically harm her again. Tara with tears streaming down her face just nodded and hoped this time his promise would reign true.

*   *   *

Patrick didn't understand what was going on inside of him. Tara was one of the few women in his life whom he truly loved and could really trust. Yet, it seemed lately he was always hurting her. That bothered him. He knew he had to get help before he truly lost control. It was like he was annoyed that Tara was so heavily dependent on him. Yet, at the same time that's what he loved most about her. Not that she was helpless, but that she was so determined to be independent even after the accident. His friends teased him about Tara; they called her the "wingless bird." Patrick knew he could have any woman he wanted. He had the looks, the smarts, and the finances to wine and dine the best of them, but to him Tara was the best. She was smart, sassy, and sexy. He knew he was in love with her, but lately her constant nagging and his outrageous temper had him questioning his feelings.

Everyone except Tara knew about Patrick's business. He worked very hard to keep her in the dark. His trade, although illegal, had been providing for his mother, sister, and brother ever since he was sixteen years old. Patrick had decided early on that he didn't want to sell drugs for his entire life. He had a plan; his goal was to legitimize. His first step at age nineteen was to buy his first house which he signed over to his mother and siblings. Then, he started to invest in other properties around the city. Now at twenty-eight, he owned two condos, one apartment building, and one laundry mat. With the income from his real estate investments alone, he could have retired from the drug life. Yet, his life wasn't turning out the way he had planned.   He felt like he was trapped - in too deep to get out of the game.   And all his feelings of anger and disappointment were being hurled directly at Tara.

*   *   *

"Tara, honey...I keep telling you that you don't have to stay with him. Come on home. This is where you belong. If I told your father about this, he would kill that boy," Tara's mother said as she tried to talk sense into her daughter's head, but it just seemed like good sense didn't live there any more.

"I know Ma, but you are wrong. I do belong here," Tara replied.

Tara's mother began to lose her patience. "No child, where you belong," she stated while switching the receiver into her other hand to get a better grip on the phone, "is with family who love and care for you. Where you belong is with someone who loves you and treats you with respect."

Tara snapped, "I am with someone who treats me with love and respect."

"Tara!   Tell me how pushing you out of a wheelchair can be characterized as treating you with love or respect?" her mother snapped back.

"I knew I shouldn't have told you. Look, Ma I got to go." Tara said as she twisted the phone cord in her hand.

Concerned, Tara's mother asked softly, "How do you expect me to respond, Sugar? You are the only daughter I have and your father and I...well, we both love you and we don't want you to get hurt. We have raised you to be a self-sufficient, responsible, and intelligent young lady. You do know you have options, right?"

"I know Ma. Listen, I have to go."

"Tara?"

"Yes, Ma."

"I want you to read Psalm Ninety-one. We are praying for you, Baby."

"Yeah Ma, I know. Bye!" Tara said quickly as she hung up the phone.

Tara knew she should not have told her mother about this last incident with Patrick, but her mother was the only person she could share her secrets with – both good and bad. Tara was in love with Patrick and it wasn't that butterfly in your stomach kind of love. This was true, Godly love and she knew it - even if no one else did, including Patrick. Tara believed that God had a special purpose for her and Patrick. She tried talking to Patrick about God, but he just wouldn't listen.

Tara thought back to the night when she had almost lost her life in the car accident with the drunk driver. Although she survived the crash, Tara's road to recovery had been extremely difficult. Patrick was with her every step of the recovery process. He became her best friend, lover, and protector. Against her parents' wishes, Tara had moved out of her cramped apartment into Patrick's condo. She wondered if she had made the right decision and if her feelings for him had grown more intense because of the accident. Tara knew that she was extremely dependent on him. Unfortunately, her conversation with her Mom had only vexed her more, and she was just as perplexed about her situation as before. Tara could still hear her mother's words replaying over and over again in her mind,

"Tell me how pushing you out of your wheelchair can be characterized as love or respect!"

Tara wasn't anyone's dummy; the car accident definitely had not injured her brain. She had always told herself that she would never put up with abuse of any kind from anyone. Yet, she wondered if maybe she was subjecting herself to Patrick's abuse for fear of losing him – fear that no other guy would want the burden of a wheelchair-bound girlfriend. Although the doctors assured Tara that the damage to the nerves in her legs was temporary, she worried about her future.

Tara rolled her wheelchair from the kitchen to the bedroom and reached for the Bible on the nightstand. She turned the well-worn pages to Psalm Ninety-one; it was her and her mother's favorite.

"He who dwells in the shelter of the Most High will rest in the shadow

of the Almighty. I will say of the Lord, 'He is my refuge and my fortress, My God, in whom I trust."

Tara remembered when her mother used to read this scripture to her as a child. She closed her eyes and recited the rest from memory.

"Surely he will save me from the fowler's snare and from the deadly pestilence. He will cover me with his feathers, and under his wings I will find refuge; His faithfulness will be my shield and rampart. I will not fear the terror of night, nor the arrow that flies by day, nor the pestilence that stalks in the darkness, nor the plague that destroys at midday. A thousand may fall at my side, ten thousand at my right hand, but it will not come near me. With my eyes I will observe and see the punishment of the wicked, but it shall not come near me. Because I have made the Lord, who is my refuge, even the Most High, my dwelling place, no evil shall befall me, nor shall any plague come near my dwelling; For He shall give His angels charge over me to keep me in all my ways. In their hands they shall bear me up lest I dash my foot against a stone. I shall tread upon the lion and the cobra. The young lion and the serpent I shall trample underfoot. Because I have set my love upon God, he will deliver me. He will set me on high because I have known His name. I shall call upon God and He will answer me. God will be with me in trouble. He will deliver me and honor me. With long life, He will satisfy me and show me His salvation."

Tara's mother had taught her long ago how to personalize the Word. As she drifted into a deep sleep that Word became part of her dreams.

*   *   *

The Rev. Tracey Javon Talby pastored the New Hope Church of God in one of the worst neighborhoods in Baltimore City. Rev. Talby and his wife had moved only a block away from the church against the wishes of both their families and, surprisingly enough, a few of their most dedicated church members. Like most churches in Baltimore, New Hope's membership was not based in the neighborhood surrounding the church, but in nearby counties. Rev. Talby felt this abandonment of the City by the more economically inclined was a serious problem and a major factor in the city's neglect. He hoped his decision to move into the neighborhood would encourage members of his congregation to do the same.

It hadn't been easy convincing his wife, Lacey, five years ago that he had needed to quit his $65,000 good government job to heed God's call full-time. And it definitely wasn't easy convincing her that he had heard God telling him to sell their $350,000 five bedroom house in Carroll County to move into a newly renovated $60,000 three-bedroom row house in a section of East Baltimore called Zombie Land. The name had originally been coined by a local newspaper for the large number of addicts who openly walked the streets in search of drugs. At one point, Rev. Talby thought Lacey would surely leave him. They had many heated debates about the move; he saw the fear and anger in Lacey's eyes during each and every one of those exchanges. And although she was clear on her concerns and her wishes to stay where they were, she stuck by his side. Rev. Talby loved Lacey for truly believing in him and trusting his decision.

*   *   *

The pearl white Lincoln Navigator cruised to its destination with its driver lost in thought. Patrick couldn't seem to focus on the deal he was about to complete; his thoughts were on Tara. He felt horrible about the way he had treated her. He hadn't intended on pushing her out of her wheelchair. He was losing control, and he didn't know what to do. After circling the block a second time, he spotted the gray Mercedes with the tinted windows as it pulled in front of the church. Patrick parked a block short of the church to wait out his next move. He had learned a long time ago that hasty actions could get a man killed. Patience was one good trait this game had taught him; he just wished he had more of it with Tara. Just as he reached for his cell phone to alert the driver of the Mercedes of his whereabouts, the church doors swung open. A young man dressed in baggy jeans and Timberlands walked down the stairs and made his way over to the Mercedes. Patrick froze. He put down his phone knowing there was no way he was going to go through with the transaction now. He also knew that he should probably split the scene, but for some reason he rolled down his window just enough to hear the exchange between the two men.

The guy with the baggy jeans walked over to the gray Mercedes with his hands in the air and his head tilted toward the closed window and asked, "Hey man, how you doing?"

The Mercedes' window came down a bit and in almost a growl

someone responded, "What?"

The guy spoke again in a casual tone, "I asked how you are doing."

"You need something fool?" the voice in the Mercedes responded.

"I need you to respect the House of the Lord. I am expecting church members to roll up any minute for choir rehearsal. I mean no disrespect to you, but you can't do this business in front of my Father's house."

"Whatever, I don't need this s---!" came the reply from the driver as he started his engine and pulled out onto the street.

As the gray Mercedes sped away, Patrick watched the young man with the baggy jeans walk up and down the street in front of the church muttering something that was incomprehensible from where he sat in the Navigator. He watched the young man pick up the trash and drug paraphernalia that littered the ground in front of the church. He watched as two, four, six, and then a total of fifteen cars pull up. And he watched as they all disappeared behind the enormous red doors of the church.

As if snapping out of a trance, Patrick started the Navigator and steered it down the street. He paused hesitantly in front of the church. Unsure as to what he was waiting for, Patrick sat still. It wasn't long before he heard the music.

> *"Oh, it is Je-sus, oh it is Je-sus,*
> *it's Je-sus in my soul.*
> *For I have touch-ed the hem of His gar-ment,*
> *and his love has made me whole."*

It was the chords from the organ that captured Patrick's attention; it was the singer's song that captured his heart. The intensity of her voice reminded him of the way his grandmother used to sing around the house when he was a child. Sitting in the middle of the street with the engine still running, Patrick was overwhelmed with emotion as he listened as the choir repeated the verse.

> *"Oh it is Je-sus, oh it is Je-sus,*

it's Je-sus in my soul.
For I have touch-ed the hem of His gar-ment,
and his love has made me whole."

With a tingling sensation filling his gut and chest, Patrick laid his head against the headrest, closed his eyes, and listened to the singer's testimony.

"I tr-i-ed all that I could,
seem-ed like no-thing did me any good.
Then, I heard Je-sus.
He was pas-sing by,
and I de-ci-ded to give him a try."

Patrick had never tried Jesus. Whenever Tara had asked him to pray with her, he had pushed her way. In all honesty, Patrick had never felt a reason to pray because he never believed God cared much about him or his family. If God really cared, why didn't he make his life better? Better yet, why would God allow him to keep hurting Tara?

As the choir joined in and the organist piped the chords, Patrick sat lost in thought. The song had stirred something in him. He tasted the salt of his tears before he realized he was crying. Unaware that the young man with the baggy jeans had been watching him from atop the church stairs, Patrick was caught off guard by the sound of the man's voice at his driver's side window.

"Hey man, how you doing?" the young man with the baggy jeans asked as he gazed intently at Patrick through the half-down window.

"Hey...I got something in my eye," was all Patrick managed to say.

The young man eyed him curiously. "I'm Rev. Talby, the pastor of this church," he said while extending his hand to Patrick.

Patrick who wasn't interested in holding a conversation didn't offer his hand in return and replied, "Yeah, I'm Patrick."

"Well, we're just finishing choir rehearsal. You're welcome to come inside. Are you waiting for someone?"

"Naw, like I said I stopped to get something out of my eye," Patrick mumbled as he looked away from Rev. Talby.

"Well, God always has an open door for you."

"Yeah, I heard that before," Patrick said looking directly at Rev. Talby.

"Heard what?" asked Rev. Talby.

"Nothing."

"Well, I think you just missed your man," Rev. Talby said cautiously, "You know the fellow with the gray Mercedes?"

"What?" Patrick said glaring at Rev. Talby like he had just crossed the line.

"Nothing...Listen, I'm here almost seven days a week. Here's my card with my numbers. I want you to give me a call if you ever need to talk," Rev. Talby responded. He leaned closer to the window and whispered, "I can see something is troubling you, Patrick. You can sit there and pretend like you are wiping something out your eyes or you can turn your eyes toward the One who can really help you."

Patrick sighed, "Look, man I'm not for this. Thanks for the card, but I'll pass on the sermon." Just as Patrick reached to roll up his window, Rev. Talby slid a small Bible through the driver's side window and headed back up the steps.

*   *   *

Dr. Lacey Talby loved the Lord and her husband in that order. A pastor's wife was one full time job she had never expected. After completing medical school, Lacey moved to Baltimore to work for one of the most prestigious hospitals in the world. If you had asked her seven years ago who she would have married, Lacey's answer definitely would not have been the pastor of a church in a neighborhood that housed almost seventy-five percent of the paraplegic, gun-shot victims she doctored. And if anyone had told her that she and her husband would live in that same neighborhood, she probably would have laughed.

She thought back to the day she had met her husband in the very same hospital where she now worked. He was there visiting one of her patients. A third year resident, Lacey had just stepped into the doorway of the room with the lead physician when she heard someone praying with such force that it stopped her in her tracks. When the prayer ended, Lacey walked into the room only to see a brother so fine that she lost herself in the deep of his big brown eyes. She was surprised to learn that this fine brother was not just a good prayer, but a good pastor, as well. After an intense five month courtship, Lacey accepted the offer to become the wife of the Rev. Tracey Javon Talby.

Lacey called the courtship intense because she had never met a man before who touched the core of her soul so completely. Javon, as she liked to call him, was honest and to the point; he seemed to know what she needed even better than she did. And he turned her on in every way imaginable. Lacey had never had such strong feelings for a man without having first crossed that sexual threshold. She had had her share of one night stands, and she had lost her naivety years ago, but something about the Rev. Tracey Javon Talby made Lacey lose every ounce of coolness and resolve that she worked years to exhibit in the presence of fine black men. She realized early on that her practiced reserve was no match for him for Javon approached her in every way opposite any man she had ever met. On their first date, they had gone to the mall, eaten dinner at a Tai restaurant, and gone jogging afterward. All of their dates were like this – fun, care-free, and safe. They spent the bulk of their time together discussing the latest political fiasco or the decline in the economy or contrasting their perspectives on God. They both were extremely outspoken and passionate about their feelings for each other and the Lord. Lacey had asked God for direction in the relationship and believed Javon was the man that God had ordained for her life. She wasn't the least bit surprised when he proposed to her a few months later.

*   *   *

Patrick sat on the couch thumbing through the little Bible that

Rev. Talby had given him. The book didn't make much sense to him, and he became frustrated as he tried to figure out all of the stories and scriptures that didn't seem to have much meaning or connection to his life. Just as Patrick was about to place the book into his briefcase, Rev. Talby's business card fell onto the floor. As he bent over to pick up the card, Patrick thought back to the day he met Rev. Talby. The dude didn't seem like the average preacher. As a matter of fact, he didn't look much older than him. After a moment or so, Patrick decided to call Rev. Talby and take him up on his offer. Patrick wondered if Rev. Talby might be able to shed some light on why he kept so much anger bottled up inside and why it all seemed to be directed toward Tara. He hesitated before reaching for the phone but dialed the number anyway.

"This is Rev. Talby, how can I be of service to you?" asked the voice on the other end of the receiver.

Patrick hadn't expected Rev. Talby to answer the phone. He thought for sure he would get a recorded message or an assistant.

"Hello...is anyone there?" came the response from the other end of the line.

"Yeah, Rev. Talby...this is Patrick. I met you..."

Before he could finish, Rev. Talby interjected, "Sure, you're the brother with the bad eyes."

Patrick laughed and responded in a serious voice, "Look Rev, this is totally new for me. My fiancé is the praying one, not me. I know I need a change in my life. I know I love my fiancé, and I know she loves me. I also know she loves God. I never thought this God thing was for me, but I wondered if it...I mean if my fiancé's faith could be so strong...can it be just as strong for me? Why should I place my faith in God? I mean...does God even care about me?"

Rev. Talby took a deep breath, "Patrick, God is available to everyone. He just asks that we open our hearts to Him. I tell you what why don't you and your fiancé stop by the church next Tuesday around 7:00 p.m. My wife and I host a weekly couple's ministry. We should be wrapping up just about that time. The two of us can sit down and talk with you two together or individually...whichever you prefer. And maybe I can answer some more of your questions about God?"

"Well, my fiancé is in a wheelchair and if I remember correctly we might have some difficulty maneuvering ourselves up those stairs," Patrick replied wearily.

"Well," Rev. Talby said, "we have a side entrance around the corner from where you were parked the other night that accommodates wheelchairs. Once inside, we have elevators and lots of open space, so she should be fine."

"Cool, I'll think on it."

"Great. Is there anything else bothering you, Patrick?"

Patrick hesitated before replying, "Naw, it's all good. I'll definitely think about stopping by next week with my girl. Peace, Rev."

                    *   *   *

"Excuse me, Dr. Talby. Your 2:00 p.m. appointment is here," Lacey's assistant announced through the intercom breaking her train of thought.

"Great, send her in," Lacey replied. She stood up and walked around the desk to greet her new patient.

Tara rolled slowly into the office and said flatly, "Hi, I'm Tara Mackrall."

"Well, Ms. Mackrall, I'm Dr. Talby, and we have a lot to talk about, but I wondered if we could pray first?"

Tara looked directly into Dr. Talby's eyes and smiled. As she reached for Dr. Talby's hands, Tara said, "Sure. I could really use some help from God right now."

Dr. Talby gave Tara a reassuring smile, took her hands into her own, and interceded on her behalf.

"Lord, you are so awesome and great. Your Word tells us that you are our healer and protector. Your Word also tells us that all things are possible through our faith in you. Lord, we come before you today with strong faith and a strong mind. We stand in great expectation for Tara's total restoration and healing. Guide her through this journey. Guide me as I shepherd healing and good health to her body and mind. Lord, let the freedom of your Holy Spirit rest upon Tara and those in her immediate circle of support. Open their hearts and minds to a new revelation of you as they accompany Tara on her journey to wellness. Give them strength and patience. Send your angels to encourage, comfort, and protect them. And let your perfect will be done. In Jesus name we pray, Amen."

Neither of them knew the power of that one prayer, nor could they have ever imagined the impact it would have on the lives of the two men whom they loved.

Liberation Letter #2

Dear Self,

I looked into the mirror this morning and despised the woman that peered back at me.   I hated the worn out gaze of her eyes, the frown of her brow, and the flat appearance of her face. As I looked into the mirror at the dim reflection of myself, I started to cry. I tried to wipe away the tears, but they continued to fall as I began babbling to myself...to that dark image in front of me and finally to God. When it felt like I had lost it, I realized that in my moment of total surrender I had actually gained it all. I felt the peace of God hovering around me - loving me, healing me, empowering me.   I heard a voice whisper, *"And this too shall pass."* And my mind remembered His Word...*"there is no place His Spirit cannot go and even when the darkness hides me, God's light becomes night around me. His Holy Spirit is there to comfort and guide me."* And I realize that I just needed to let God in. So I did, and I found myself.

And this evening as I look back into the mirror at the reflection of the woman before me, I see hope. I see a twinkle in her eyes, a glow on her face, and a light in her smile. I see the me God meant the world to see. The me - who has forgiven herself and released her burdens. The me - who has sought God's forgiveness, accepted His salvation, and received His grace. I look at me in the mirror and smile because I understand that I am finally FREE!

Love Always,
God's Daughter

There

There she was
sitting pretty
hoping for a compliment
that would never come.

There she was
standing tall
seeking acceptance and recognition
for a work
that would never be done.

There she was
running fast from her problems
and blinding herself
in a false sense of security.

And there was God
all-knowing,
all-seeing,
omnipotent,
and divine
waiting for her to surrender it all to Him.

Hallelujah!

Woke up this morning with a smile on my face
came to work and that smile was quickly erased.

You see the enemy was there
planning, scheming, and conniving.

What he didn't know or truly understand
was that the God in me is bigger than any of his plans.

What he failed to realize
without a doubt
is that this sister is crazy sold out!

No weapon formed against me shall prosper!
No good thing will be denied from me!
I am a righteous daughter walking in victory!

I stared the enemy straight in his ugly face
and stood firm as I handled my business with grace!

I can walk away with my dignity intact
a smile on my face and with no regrets.

While the enemy sits back
and wonders in a haze
trying to figure out
how I am still here...
head held high
and walking
with a vibrant praise!

My Thanksgiving Prayer

God, I thank you for waking me up this morning.
I thank you for your continued grace and mercy.
I thank you for the comfort of your love and your Holy Spirit.
I thank you for keeping and protecting me and comforting me.
I thank you for the peace of your forgiveness.
I thank you for new beginnings.

Lord, I thank you for helping me understand
that my past does not dictate my future.
I thank you for showing me that no matter what others may think about me
or feel about me that what ultimately matters is how I feel about myself.
I thank you for providing your Word and
providing your shepherds to teach and guide me.

Lord, I thank you for giving me a new day to right the wrongs of yesterday.
I thank you for loving me, and I thank you for showing me how to love me.
I thank you for my growth in this Christian walk.
I thank you for preparing my heart for life affirming change.
I thank you for liberating my mind and my soul.
I thank you God for setting me free!
I thank you for releasing the fear, the hurt, the doubt, and the pain.
I thank you for releasing me from the disappointment,
the self-loathing, and the shame.

Lord, I thank you for giving me your favor and blessings.
I thank you for the trials in my life;
they have taught me resilience and strength.
I thank you for your Word and its affirming power and grace.

The Place that Seems Like the End is Only the Beginning: Journal Entries from the Heart

<u>The Man</u>

I miss you. I miss your presence and I miss the freedom of knowing that I can be with you. To be honest, I began to miss you as I walked away from you, but I was too stubborn too admit it to myself. A man's silly pride can make him do silly things. But whatever happens, I just don't want to lose you. I never would have imagined that in such a short period of time, you could mean so much to me...imagine that. Today is Memorial Day, and I just want to be where you are.

<u>The Woman</u>

I believe you really care for me, and I've been thinking of you constantly since we were last together. I wonder why I have not heard from you and realize you left town without telling me. I keep replaying that last night we were together in my head asking myself whether I said or did anything to trigger your flight. You see, it's been such a long time since I have been in a healthy relationship that I'm not sure what to do or expect. I do know that getting to know you over these past few weeks have really meant so much to me. I think you said it best, "who would have thought you would mean so much to me in so little time." Well, the feeling is mutual. I know it's too soon for me to feel this way, but you came into my life at a time when it seemed like all hell was breaking loose, and the decisions I made were in response to all of the drama and not in response to what God would have had me to do. Somehow, I feel that God put you on my path. The time I have spent with you has nurtured my spirit. You have captured my heart in so many ways that I can't even begin to explain. I know there is so much more that we still have to learn about each other, but I hope we have the opportunity to hold onto whatever it is that we have, right now, and to make it into a lifetime of something beautiful.

<u>The Man</u>

I feel schizophrenic. One minute, I'm sure you're the one I want and the next minute I'm wondering if you're just a distraction from the loneliness of losing her. She called and I jetted. And although you are different from anyone I have ever met, you are not her. Still, I can't seem to get you out of my head. Your smell, your smile, your voice keep me coming back. I am torn. I care for you, but I don't think I love you. In fact, you scare me. I'm not sure why, but a part of me wants to run as far as I can away from you. Yet, another part of me wants to hold you in my arms forever.

The Man

I drove past your place last night. It was pretty late, and I didn't see your car. I can't believe I'm back to this again. Even though we have spent an enormous amount of time together during these last few weeks, I must admit that I don't really know that much about you. I do know that we are from two different worlds. I hate yours. My cousin warned me about you. He said, "A woman like that is looking to live off you." I can't get his words out of my head, but each day I get to know you I am intrigued by your determination and stamina to succeed. I keep asking God what is it about you that keep me coming back. You don't fit the mode, so why am I drawn to you? It's not the sex, since we haven't crossed that bridge, yet. Well, not entirely anyway. And, still I can't get you out of my head.

The Woman

I try to eliminate you from my thoughts, but I can't seem to get you off my mind. I have thought a lot about what you said to me during our last conversation. I think about how you were ready to end our relationship because I pushed you sexually to a place you told me you weren't ready to go with me. That's a first! I don't think I ever had a guy break up with me because I wanted to have sex with him. Isn't it supposed to be the other way around? And although I was hurt and angry at your rejection, I was somewhat ashamed of my actions. It made me question my own walk as a Christian.

The Woman

I miss you so much. And like it or not, you bring out all my insecurities. When I first met you it was right at the time I felt like all hope was lost in me finding a man like you. I want you, but I'm always so tense around you. It's like I'm afraid that I won't ever measure up, but again that's how I have always felt with every man in my life. I believe it is because I felt that way with my father...like I could never get it right.

The Woman

It has finally occurred to me that what we had is no longer. Yet, I continue to write. I write knowing now that you will never understand the true meaning of my heart. Still, I cannot stop this endless stream of words. I think of you often...of your smile...and that intense gaze. The hardest part of all of this is that my feelings for you have not changed although our relationship has. In my attempt to rationalize the situation I tell myself it is no more, but I wonder if I am a hundred percent sure. I ask myself how I would respond if you showed up on my doorstep. How could I turn you away? How could I resist your smile? I ask myself these questions and realize that I am unable to answer them. My heart rejects the notion of not being with you. Yet, I wonder if it's really just a rejection of the loneliness I feel in your absence.

The Man

I will probably marry her, but I can't get you out of my mind. I still don't understand you. I can't seem to control you or my feelings for you. I want to tame you, protect you, and make your life better. I keep trying to rationalize your situation. Your telephone is disconnected...that's a red flag right there. The last time we spoke you told me you had quit your job just as I told you I got a new one. My cousin's words about you being a gold digger echo in my ear, and I realize I don't trust you. Why do you live in that neighborhood? I can't understand why you won't do more to make your life better. Then it occurs to me that I am angry at you for being you. I become angry at myself for getting involved with you. Yet, I still want to see you. I need to feel you in my arms.

The Woman

And it happened just as I knew it would. I heard the constant banging on my door and turned over with each persistent knock. The urgency of the knocking had me wondering if possibly a family member was in need; it woke me and everyone else up in the building. When I finally opened the door and looked into your eyes, I wasn't prepared for the thud of my heart. In all honesty, I didn't know what to do. I was so confused. One part wanting to reach out and touch you and the other wanting to hurt you the way you had hurt me. So we sat outside my door in the hallway on the steps talking for what seemed like hours. I tried to listen. I tried really hard to simmer the growing fire in my heart. With each of your passing words, I tried to hear what you were saying to me. I don't know what I heard. I couldn't understand what you were trying to tell me. You talked about an old girlfriend, one of those model types, that you used to date and you said you realized that I was more of what you wanted. You talked about my shortfalls, and what else did you say? How did I end up in your arms? How did you end up in my bed? I think between kisses I asked you to leave. How was it that you were, suddenly, so tired to make your forty minute drive home? I realize that you are my weakness and now that you know it, I struggle with what's next.

The Woman

So you left and arrived, unannounced, two days later. We went to an evening service at my church, but you were distant and cold. Your cell phone started ringing like crazy. When you drove me home, you half-heartedly said, "I don't know. I'll talk with you soon." Hmmm, I don't remember asking you a question. Anyway, you told me you were going to see your uncle. That is what you said, right? I reached out to give you a key. But I saw that look on your face. What was it? Disgust? No; it was contempt. You laughed. No, it was more like a chuckle and I realized I am the lone lover in this affair.

The Woman

So I wait. I wait for you to show up again - unannounced and unscheduled as usual. I wonder how I am back at this point. Why is it that I always end up being the "other" woman? Isn't that what I hated about all those other relationships? I thought this one was going to be different. Where had I gone wrong? How did I become one of those silly women that my pastor preached about? I tried to respond to you like a Christ filled woman, not a sex craved little girl. I keep praying and hoping that I will be better prepared for our next encounter. I pray that with each new opportunity to see you that I will act more responsibly. I hope to think with my head and not my heart. I hope to act with courage and to walk in faith. Nonetheless, whenever you come around, my flesh takes over, and I seem to lose all the good sense that God gave me.

The Woman

You knocked although you had a key.   Then, you acted as if you didn't want me to touch you. I don't understand why I keep putting up with this torture. I'm regretting that I even gave you a key.   We had another of your conversations about your ex-girlfriend. I listened to you tell me that you needed space.   You stayed the night and although we still have never crossed that sexual barrier being in your arms took me there never the less. I left you in my bed as I dressed for work, and I left that morning with a false sense of hope. I kick myself at my stupidity and wonder if I am so desperate for a man that I will let you come and go as you please.   Come and go in and out of my life with no real respect or regard for me.

The Man

She found out about you.   At first I didn't care because I thought you had my heart, but common sense kicked in.   She is financially secure; you are not.   She is beautiful; you are beautiful with effort. She is emotionally and physically stable on every level; you are unbalanced at times. She gave me an ultimatum. I can't risk losing her. You - I don't believe I ever truly had you...so I know I will get over it. And although I enjoyed our time together, everything about you annoys me.   Why is that?   I think it is because I always felt you weren't good enough for me.   And the other week when you refused to let me stay overnight at your place, you pissed me off. I don't need you, but I do need her.

The Woman

I called you because I couldn't wait another minute another hour or another day for you to call me.   And when you answered the phone, you were just as cold as I suspected you would be.   I invited you to a crab feast and it was like De Ja Vu. You asked me if you could stay with me because you had an interview in town the next day. I said no. I called you the following night to see how your interview went and it was as if you were a complete stranger.   My depression about you heightens all of my old insecurities. The fact that I am without a secure job and living in an apartment without basic utilities doesn't help the situation. I wanted more than life to let you stay with me when you asked, but I knew if you saw my current state of living what little ounce of respect you had for me would be lost forever.   I question my sanity.   Here I am sitting in the dark in a half-empty apartment worrying over a man who ain't much worried about me. I think I have lost my mind.

The Woman

The sun set last night and rose this morning, and I am still here. That realization helps me understand that the mess I'm in will eventually pass if I just keep moving and not focus on it. So I continue to move forward. I get up everyday and work two part-time jobs. Yet, I am unable to make enough money to pay my rent, my car payment, or my insurance. So, I ask myself why I am working if not to pay bills. The answer is clear; work keeps me sane. Thus, I keep working...while trying to figure out how to get out of this mess. I mull over what I'm supposed to be doing in the meantime. And I realize that you are still very much a part of my thoughts. So, I call you one last time. To be truthful, I have been trying to call you for weeks. I finally mustered the courage to leave you a message. You know it never occurred to me that I didn't have anything other than a cell phone number for you. It never entered my mind that all those conversations about your ex-girlfriend could have possibly been about your wife. I try to analyze the situation and don't understand why I continue to put out and refuse to put in. I ponder why it seems that I value others more than I value myself. I wonder what is wrong with me. I cry out to God in anguish as I spiral into a dark pit of depression.

The Man

Believe it or not, I am a praying man. So know that I have prayed long and hard regarding what I am about to say. I am in love with you. I know it doesn't make sense, but I am in love with you. I saw you the other day; you didn't see me. You had that smile on your face and that sparkle I love so much in your eyes. I wondered who put it there. That one thought alone challenged me. I mean why should that matter to me? Why should I care? I had already come to the conclusion that you were not the one for me, right? After seeing you that day, I went to be with my fiancée and realized that she is a weak substitute for you. So with a wedding scheduled in six weeks, I awkwardly tell her that I need more time and space. I tell her that I am not ready for this commitment thing, but deep in my heart I know that I am ready to commit, just not with her.

The Woman

It's been twelve months, two weeks, and six days since you left. I thank God that I made it through the loss of you - wiser and whole. Your leaving forced me to deal with me. This year has been so very difficult, but praise God I survived. You see, I have learned to love me, appreciate me, and value everything that is part of me. Most importantly, I have learned to cast my cares on the Lord. I focus on the little things, the daily blessings. I take small steps and it seems to be working. I have a new job, a new car, and a new perspective on life. I've learned that the people in my life won't change, but I can change my attitude toward them and toward myself. I continue to pray and study God's Word. I realize that it is the love of God that is keeping me alive. I mean truly alive and I trust in His will for my life. I won't pretend that everyday has been easy, and I won't even bog you down with the details of the bad mistakes and misjudgments that I have made along the way. What I will tell you though is how God brought me through. It's like for the first time I'm on the outside looking in. I can feel me growing, evolving, and becoming the woman that God has ordained me to be. Yet, I'm still alone. Sometimes my mind drifts back to you, and I savor the moment - the sweet memories - of what used to be. But then I snap back into reality, and I realize that my future is greater than any experience of my past. So, I wait in great expectation for the King God is preparing for me.

The Man

The day came when the two of us were finally in the same place at the same time. I knew it would happen eventually. I mean this town isn't but so big, but isn't it funny that we would bump into each other at the same mall where we had our first date. There you were head bent, mind racing as you studied a pair of Liz Claiborne boots. I watched you for what seemed like an eternity - studying your gaze, the tilt of her head, and the arch in your back. You looked great. I didn't expect you to look up so suddenly and turn my way. And I certainly didn't expect you to give me that beautiful smile.

The Woman

I saw you and for a moment all time stopped. For a split second, I thought about acting like I didn't see you. I have done that many times before to the men in my life who have hurt me most. When I saw them I would just look straight through them refusing to acknowledge their presence - getting my own twisted revenge for my shattered heart.   Silly, right...but it was my way of overcoming the pain of rejection.   When I saw you, the old memories of rejection and hurt began immediately to cast shadows of doubt in my mind. But a voice spoke peace to my heart and calmness to my spirit.   It reminded me that goodness and grace were in me and that I was a daughter of the Most High.   So, when I looked up and saw you gazing at me, I smiled.   It wasn't one of those phony smiles or even a nervous smile, but a true smile from one of God's daughters.

The Man

I didn't expect that.   I probably could have handled it better if you were just rude to me.   If you had rolled your eyes at me or turned away from me, I probably could have used that as an excuse to justify all of the pain I've caused you.   If you had ignored me, I could have dismissed the love I still hold for you.   Yet, once again you captured my heart, and I was ill prepared for the light and warmth that resonated from you.   I was even less prepared for this chance encounter with the more mature and whole you.   Yet, there you were before me.   And, there I was for the first time praying for both you and me.   There I was asking God to show me how to open my heart to you. There I was asking God to show me how to love you.

THE END

Book Club and/or Study Group Discussion Questions

The author would love to hear from you. Please email your comments and/or reactions to lpinder@thetakeactionnetwork.com. Additionally, please feel free to use the following set of questions as talking points for your Book Club, Study Group, and/or Reading Circle discussions:

1. What is a psalm? What is the significance of the book of *Psalms* in The Holy Bible? Why do you think the author named this collection of poems and short stories, Psalms of the Daughter?

2. In the story, "Closure," the main character struggles to overcome the guilt of having an abortion. What is the significance of this story's title? Using scripture as your reference, do you think God has a position on abortion?

3. Do you believe that satan/the adversary/devil/demon and/or evil spirits really exist? Discuss some instances in The Holy Bible where individuals had to face satan/demons/ and/or evil spirits.

4. The book of *Acts* in The Holy Bible provides multiple examples of God's spirit making bold witnesses out of ordinary people. In the story, "Acts," do you think God used any of the characters to make a bold witness? If so, explain which ones and describe how.

5. In the story, "Jewel," one of the main characters is affected with AIDS, one of the leading causes of death in Black women. Has HIV/AIDS impacted your life in anyway? How might the church and/or faith-based organizations help raise awareness about the issue of AIDS and/or HIV?

6. In the story, "Salvation," the characters face a variety of social issues (i.e. disability, domestic abuse/violence, drugs). Do you believe that social issues - like domestic abuse/violence - are prevalent in the church? Do you believe that the church has a role in helping to resolve social issues? Why or why not?

7. The last story in the collection describes an intense love affair between an un-named man and woman. What were some of the major conflicts in the story? What is your position on Christian Dating? Do you think proper boundaries were in place to support a healthy, Christian relationship between the two characters? Why or why not?

8. The author sectioned Psalms of the Daughter into three chapters with corresponding themes and biblical scriptures. Discuss how you think the different stories and poems relate to the corresponding themes and biblical scriptures listed on each chapter page.

9. Do you feel Psalms of the Daughter could be used as an effective ministry tool? Why or why not?

TAKE ACTION! Publishing

TAKE ACTION! Publishing, a project of The TAKE ACTION! Network, and a subsidiary of Create-A-Book BALTIMORE was created to,

- help aspiring and seasoned authors use online resources to print Christian-themed works of fiction and non-fiction.

- help individuals and organizations document their stories of challenge and/or triumph in taking action against social, environmental, and economic injustices.

To request submission guidelines, email a brief description of your writing project and a short bio to lpinder@thetakeactionnetwork.com. Please be sure to include your full name, telephone number, and mailing address in your email.

For additional information, visit www.takeactionpublishing.com.

Breinigsville, PA USA
24 August 2009
222874BV00006B/6/A

9 781414 101590